GOD HAS EARS

A SPIRITUAL JOURNEY

by
DOREEN PECK
with
PENELOPE YOUNG

Penelope Young Publications

© Copyright 1999

All rights reserved. No part of this publication may be reproduced, stored in a retrieval system, or transmitted, in any form or by any means, electronic, mechanical, photocopying, recording or otherwise, without the prior written permission of the publisher.

British Library Cataloguing in Publication Data.
A catalogue record for this book is available from the British Library.

ISBN 0 9527148 1 7

Published by:
Penelope Young
21 Landseer Road, Southwell,
Nottinghamshire NG25 0LX

Production by
MOORLEY'S Print & Publishing
23 Park Rd., Ilkeston, Derbys DE7 5DA
Tel/Fax: (0115) 932 0643
In association with Redwood Books
Author's typesetting supplied on disk

CONTENTS

Notes		4
Map of Rwanda & Burundi		5
Prologue		7
Chapter 1 -	'The Lord is my Shepherd, I shall not want': **Early years of life and faith**	9
Chapter 2 -	'He leads me beside the waters of rest': **Journey to Rwanda**	31
Chapter 3 -	'He makes me dwell in green pastures': **Land of hills and valleys**	45
Chapter 4 -	'He restores my soul': **Revival**	55
Chapter 5 -	'He leads me in the paths of righteousness': **New insights in Belgium**	71
Chapter 6 -	'Though I walk through the valley of the shadow of death, I will fear no evil': **Revolution and Refugees**	77
Chapter 7 -	'Thou anointest my head with oil': **Renewal**	99
Chapter 8 -	'My cup runneth over': **Widening Horizons**	117
Chapter 9 -	'Thou art with me': **Mothers' Union work**	127
Chapter 10 -	'Thy rod and thy staff they comfort me': **All Nations and beyond**	143
Chapter 11 -	'Surely goodness and mercy shall follow me': **Rwanda Revisited**	161
Chapter 12 -	'All the days of my life': **Hope for the future**	175
Epilogue -	'I shall dwell in the house of the Lord for ever'	185
Chronology		187
Bibliography		189

Note on Abbreviations:

ARM	Anglican Renewal Ministries
BCMS	Bible Churchmen's Missionary Society (now Crosslinks)
BIFCU	Bristol Inter-Faculty Christian Union
BMS	Baptist Missionary Society
CMJ	Church's Ministry among Jewish People
CMS	Church Missionary Society (now Church Mission Society)
IVF	Inter-Varsity Fellowship of Evangelical Unions (now UCCF – University and Colleges Christian Fellowship)
IVMF	Inter-Varsity Missionary Fellowship
OMF	Overseas Missionary Fellowship
SAMS	South American Missionary Society
SOMA	Sharing of Ministries Abroad
USPG	United Society for the Propagation of the Gospel

The Ruanda General and Medical Mission of CMS - later known simply as Ruanda Mission CMS - is now known as MAM (Mid-Africa Ministry)

Note on Spellings:

Ruanda and Urundi represent the old colonial spellings of these names; since Independence the two countries have been known as Rwanda and Burundi, which more closely follow the national pronunciation.

Note on Language:

Kinyarwanda - the Rwandan national language
(ki = literally 'thing of' - as in Kirundi, language of Burundi)
Munyarwanda - a Rwandan national
(umu = one person - as in Murundi, Muganda)
Banyarwanda - Rwandan people
(ba = people - as in Baganda, Bahutu)

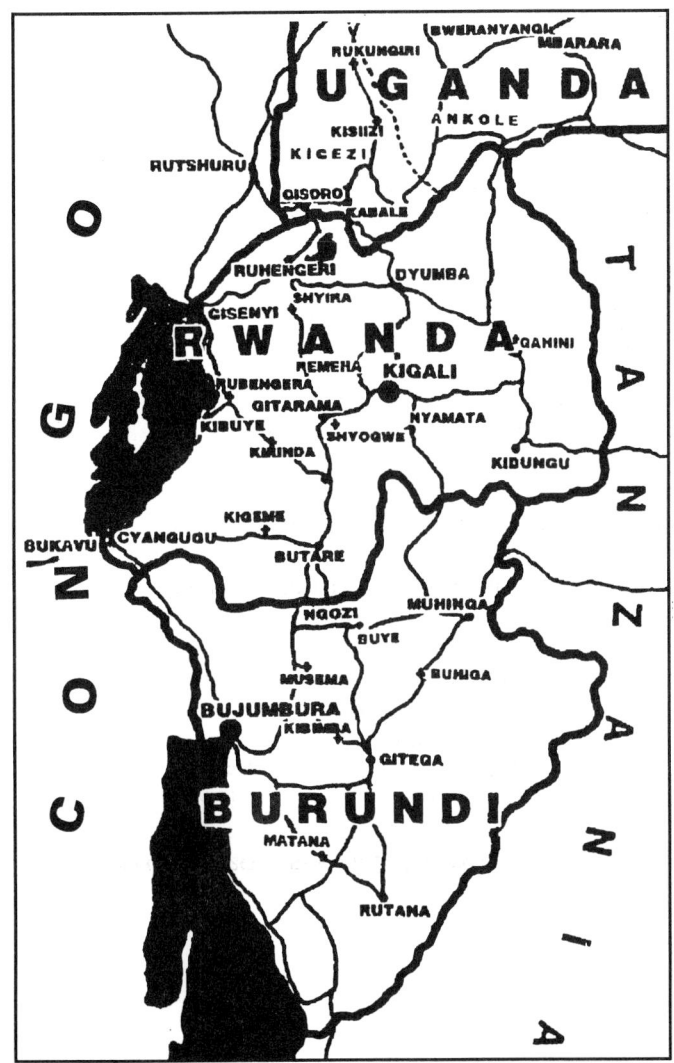

Map of S.W. Uganda, Rwanda and Burundi

Prologue

'Of making many books there is no end,' warned the Preacher in Ecclesiastes. What was true in his day is infinitely more so in ours, and I would not have thought of adding to the number but for a 'chance encounter' which I believe was God-directed.

When in 1994 the horrors of genocide brought the virtually unheard-of little country of Rwanda constantly to our television screens, I was asked by the Mission Committee of Southwell Minster to speak at one of their 'World for Christ' monthly meetings, and give some background and help towards their understanding of what underlay the ethnic strife. This was in view of my twenty-three years spent with the Anglican Church in Rwanda and Burundi, and I gladly accepted this offer. An open meeting was arranged in the church hall, to which members of other churches in Southwell also came. I showed colour transparencies and shared my experiences of 'another Rwanda' - not only the breath-taking beauty of this land, but of the warm hospitality of its people, of all ethnic groups, and especially of the faith and testimony of so many members of the Christian churches who in the past and now in these times of terrible suffering, proved that God indeed 'has ears', and that His grace really is sufficient. Thoughtful questions followed, with general discussion and prayer, then the meeting ended and I stayed behind to pack up my belongings.

Hesitating as I left the hall as to whether I should turn up into the town or return past the Minster to my car, I chose the latter. Along the path I was met by one of those who had attended the meeting, returning towards the hall. Penny Young explained how, as she was walking away from the meeting, she had felt a strong prompting to return and ask me if I would consider joining with her in the writing of a book about my Rwanda experiences. Surprised, but also excited by the suggestion, I agreed that we could meet to talk and pray about the possibility.

In thinking it over, I recognised that these amazing years in Rwanda had actually constituted only a third of my Christian life experience, and it had been just a part, although a very significant one, of my ongoing spiritual journey. I believed it was right that the book should be more of a spiritual autobiography. Consequently, Penny and I met regularly in the months ahead, she prompting with questions, directing my reminiscences and making copious notes. These she spent many hours transcribing, and I cannot adequately express my gratitude to her for her dedication and patience.

So often as I recounted incidents, sometimes inspiring, sometimes challenging and once or twice dangerous, the thought of God's open ear to our cries recurred again and again. When I first lived in Rwanda, I discovered the older people had vivid idioms for the attributes of the Almighty (recognised in pre-Christian Rwanda) - e.g. 'God has arms', i.e. He is powerful, and 'God has ears', i.e. He listens to us. So although the younger Rwandans do not seem to use this term now, I have felt I should use it for the title of this book, which is my testimony to His care, guiding, and enabling through so many years and experiences. Indeed, looking back to my non-churchgoing, rather secular upbringing, and recording just some of the steps in the pathway to Christian service in other lands, I cannot but re-echo the words which a Burundi pastor, himself from a pagan upbringing, composed for their hymn- book: 'Oh, how the Grace of God amazes me! It saved me from my sin and set me free.' This I have proved throughout my life ... to Him be the Glory!

Chapter 1
Early years of life and faith

Bells pealed out over the city of Westminster on the 5th of July, 1919, as I arrived safely in the world. It was not, however, to greet my arrival that the bells were ringing, but to commemorate the signing of the Peace Treaty between Britain and Germany seven days previously. My father, Alfred Bindley Peck, was one of the band ringing this 'Te Deum for Victory and Peace - 5040 changes of Thurstan's four-part peal of Stedman Triples, lasting three hours and eighteen minutes - which was, incidentally, the first peal to be rung on the newly cast ring of bells at Westminster Abbey.

Bell-ringing ran in my father's family; his father before him had been a bell-ringer in Bedford, and when my father moved to London he at once sought out and joined bands of ringers at various churches. Before long he was invited to join the Ancient Society of College Youths (established in 1637, London's oldest ringing Society) whose members were responsible for the ringing of the bells of St. Paul's Cathedral, Westminster Abbey and other well-known London churches. He rang for most State occasions, from Queen Victoria's Diamond Jubilee to Queen Elizabeth II's Coronation, including State Openings of Parliament, the coronations and funerals of Edward VII, George V and George VI, and several royal weddings. He received a ticket for each of the weddings. It was my turn to use the one for the wedding of Princess Marina to the Duke of Kent, and I remember climbing proudly up to my seat in the triforium above the chancel! I can still visualise the glittering spectacle below me.

My father, Alfred Bindley Peck, ringing the bells at St. Paul's Cathedral

9

A skilful 'heavy' bell-ringer, up to the time of his death my father was the only man known to have 'turned in' the tenor (that is, the heaviest) bell weighing seventy-two hundredweight at Exeter Cathedral, to a peal. He is also remembered in bell-ringing circles as the man who rang the last bell, the tenor, of the last change of Bow Bells in 1940, when a war-time ban silenced them, except as an invasion signal. A year later the bells were destroyed in the Blitz, on the night of the 10th May, 1941, when they crashed down from the high tower in the midst of the burning ruins of St. Mary-le-Bow. Medallions were cast from the metal, and I still treasure the one given to my father with his initials 'A.P.' embossed upon it.

As I grew up I was very close to my father. He taught me to play chess and to throw a cricket ball, which girls then were not supposed to be able to do properly. And I realise he instilled into me standards of honesty and 'fair play', mainly by telling instances from his own childhood such as the time when his father had made him take back to the owner some apples he had picked up from the road where they had fallen. From an early age he would take me up with him to the ringing chambers, especially St. Paul's Cathedral. I loved climbing up the 350 steps of its spiral staircase, and looking out through the apertures right across London.

From early days, therefore, I was well acquainted with churches - but only their bell towers! We never went inside the churches themselves and neither did my mother. My father was what used to be known as a 'Godfearer' - godly and upright in his living according to the ethical standards of his day, but not a regular worshipper, though he believed he did his part in calling others to church! I was fascinated by the whole 'exercise' of bell-ringing, and would have liked to learn, but women bell-ringers were virtually unheard of at that time, and besides my mother said that one bell-ringer in the family was enough. It can become a real addiction; when not at his work, my father was always off somewhere ringing bells - at weekends, evenings, and times of special festivals like Christmas and Easter - so it did have its effect on our family life. His programme on Sundays was to ring at St. Paul's at 10 am, then down the Strand to ring at St. Clement Dane's, and on to Westminster Abbey for their mid-day service. After lunch he returned to St. Paul's for early Evensong. This programme continued even after we had moved to Reigate in Surrey, with the addition that he would finish the day by ringing at St. Mary's, the parish church there. On holidays our Sundays were often shaped by visits he wanted to make to bell-towers, and sometimes when stopping in a village while the church bells were ringing he would say, 'They're one short!' - and leaving the rest of us in the car he would climb the belfry steps to join in.

When he wasn't ringing bells, my father worked with pianos. He had been a piano-maker, first at John Broadwood & Sons then at Chappell & Co., making the 'action' part of the pianos, and through this work he came to know many blind people, who came to the factories for training as piano tuners. It was through this connection that he later came to be appointed as Supervisor of piano tuners at the National Institute for the Blind (now the Royal National Institute). Shortly after his appointment, the Home Industries Department, of which the piano tuners formed a part, moved to Reigate, and we as a family moved there not long afterwards. This was a role in which my father continued for the rest of his working life. As well as negotiating contracts for blind tuners with schools, hospitals and other places, he would spend most days driving them to the various places to tune the pianos and, when necessary, taking home piano actions in need of repair in order to carry out the repairs himself. In the school holidays I would often accompany him on his visits, travelling all over Kent, Surrey, Sussex, Hampshire and London south of the Thames, which was the area he covered.

Meanwhile my mother, born Emma Willment, was pursuing her own career. Upon leaving school - the Greycoat Hospital, a famous Westminster Girls' Grammar School, which had been given its charter by Queen Anne and where my mother attained high academic standards, as I discovered when looking through her various papers after her death - she started her own secretarial business and also gave piano lessons. She had her own business card, which was not common for women at that time, and took pride in being a businesswoman. As a teenager she had been an enthusiastic supporter of the Pankhursts. Though she did not go so far with the suffragettes as to chain herself to the railings of the House of Commons, she was politically active and was a member of the 'Primrose League', a political association which supported the principles of Conservatism, formed in memory of Benjamin Disraeli, Lord Beaconsfield. Primrose Day, 19th April, was marked for many years by the wearing of a primrose emblem to commemorate the anniversary of his death in 1881. Mother told me later that she had enrolled me as a 'Primrose Bud' (a junior member of the League) when I was very young, but I don't remember anything of this though I did wear my primrose every year on Primrose Day as many people did prior to the Second World War. Later on, mother became secretary at the City Carlton Club, a leading Conservative Club in the City of London. Here she came into contact with Conservative MPs, such as Sir Winston Churchill, and had high ambitions that I would eventually become an MP - as she would like to have been herself. She said she could get me a 'safe' Conservative seat! After the City Carlton Club was destroyed during the Blitz, she worked at the Gresham, and then became secretary to a City of London stockbroker. In fact she continued travelling up to London daily until the very bad London smog of 1953 brought about her untimely death by so hampering her breathing that she collapsed, and died within a week.

With my father away so much bell-ringing and my mother at work, life at home could have been somewhat disjointed, but my maternal grandmother, in whose house we lived in Westminster, held things together, bringing up my elder sister Ruby and me with the discipline and values of the Victorian era. Ruby and I were close, in spite of the almost eleven-year age gap. She played with me a great deal, took me out in the local parks, and let me into the secrets of growing up. As a family we did go on annual holidays, to visit my father's relations in Bedford, and to Ruishton, near Taunton in Somerset, where mother's mother had grown up. We usually stayed with my great-aunt, whose husband was the village blacksmith and wheelwright, and I would spend hours watching him shoe horses and mend farm vehicles. Others of Gran's relatives were farmers in the area, and I developed a great love of the countryside - in fact I wanted to be a farmer, preferably a poultry farmer, when I grew up, but my mother said it was no career for a woman! Although she had progressive ideas about equality for women, she disapproved of what she saw as an unacademic career for her daughter, especially as I seemed to be showing ability at school. In any case, she said, they didn't have the sort of capital needed to set me up on a farm. Later, when I was called to Africa as a missionary, she said she wished she'd let me be a poultry farmer!

In spite of the close connection with church bells, religion played no part at all in our family life, though my grandmother made me say 'grace' after meals - 'Thank God for my good dinner,' which I ran seamlessly on with 'Please may I get down now?' The acknowledgement of God's presence ended there! Then, in an early Scripture lesson at primary school, we were all asked to say our favourite text. 'What's a text?' I whispered to my neighbour. 'A verse from the Bible,' she replied. 'The Bible! I don't know anything about the Bible!' 'Just say, *"The Lord is my shepherd, I shall not want. Psalm 23, verse 1",*' she whispered back. So I stood up and repeated what she had said, not understanding the wonder of the verse; but I have often marvelled since at its prophetic significance for my future life.

One evening when I was about seven years old I was watching my father make lead mouldings for a piano action he had brought home for repair. He had melted the lead in a little cauldron over the kitchen range and was transferring it to his bench to pour into the mould when the pincers he was using to hold the cauldron slipped. The boiling lead fell on the floor then splashed up over my foot and legs. Quickly he tried to brush it off, but it had begun to solidify and tore the flesh away. My grandmother rushed for butter to spread on the other burns, while my mother rushed out to the nearest phone box to call our family doctor, only to be told he was away for the weekend. I had no experience of prayer, but afterwards was told that I had cried out, 'Oh God, send a doctor!' My father dashed out and ran almost a mile to the doctor's house - to meet him just arriving home in his car, having returned unexpectedly early! He put my father in the car and drove to our house, applied picric acid to the burns, and gave instructions about the care I was to be given - bed rest and regular dressings, which my sister was delighted to do. I understood later that it was due to the prompt medical attention I received that my right foot was saved. Though I did not realise it at the time the 'God who hears' had indeed heard and answered the little girl who had as yet no knowledge of him.

My next 'spiritual' experience came about a year later. My sister Ruby occasionally attended services at a nearby church, where she belonged to the Rangers. One evening she and Victor, a boy she was dating, took me along to some special festival or other. As I sat in the church (All Saints, Pimlico, on the Thames embankment) I was conscious of a 'Presence' beyond what I could actually see or hear. I can still vividly recall that awareness and my thinking, *'There's someone here - this God-business is real!'* Later that evening, after I had gone to bed, Victor asked my mother if he could come up to say Goodnight to me. 'I saw you didn't understand what was going on in that service,' he said. 'We'll try and help you sometime, but for now I'd like to pray with you.' And he prayed in a simple and direct way that I would come into a personal knowledge of the Lord. I didn't understand what he meant, and had never heard anyone pray to God personally, but I didn't forget his words. He was only 19, and my sister broke up with him soon after, but when I think about it I'm amazed at his courage and faith to pray in that way with his girlfriend's kid sister. When that prayer was finally answered and I did come into a knowledge of the Lord as my personal

Saviour, I recalled his prayer with thanksgiving. Apart from Scripture lessons at school - for which, incidentally, I won a prize, a large black Bible inscribed, 'Awarded to Doreen Peck for proficiency in Biblical Knowledge: by the Religious Tract Society' - that was my only vital contact with the Christian faith until I reached my early teens, though for a while after my experience in All Saints Church I used to think about going into the church on my own and that perhaps the vicar would come in and I could ask him more about God. But I never actually did this.

It was the death of my grandmother when I was 13 that precipitated our move to Reigate to be nearer my father's work. This necessitated my changing schools as the journey from Reigate to London every day was not practicable. Since leaving primary school I had been a pupil at the Mary Datchelor School in Camberwell, a Girls' Public Day School founded by the Clothworkers' Company and with a high reputation for academic achievement, to which I had won a Junior County Scholarship. Getting there each day from Westminster was quite a journey: a ten-minute walk along the Embankment and over Vauxhall Bridge to catch a tram or bus to Camberwell, via the Oval Cricket Ground. Often I had to walk on my own, yet no-one thought it unwise - a striking illustration of the safety of the London streets for a teenage girl at that time!

Among my classmates I had noticed some wearing shield-shaped badges with four small red crosses on them. These girls seemed quite friendly and popular, but though curious I never liked to ask what the badges were - I was too shy. Indeed, looking back, I realise I was painfully shy and timid, though interestingly I could become quite transformed when acting a part on the stage. The prospect of changing schools and starting as the only new girl half-way through the school year terrified me. The schoolgirl stories I had read which often portrayed the bullying of new girls increased my dread of this new venture. I toyed with the idea of suicide, and began to work out how it could be brought about by means of the gas oven. Then I discovered the stove in our new house was electric! There was no-one with whom I dared to share my fears, as by now Ruby had left home for some accommodation nearer to her work in the Admiralty Chart Establishment in Cricklewood. Wonderfully, help appeared in the form of two sisters whose father worked with mine at the RNIB. They called round to ask if I would like to come with them to school on the first day of term. They were senior girls, in the 5th and 6th forms, and their offer calmed my fears and made all the difference.

How vividly I remember the mid-morning break on that first day! The Form Captain, an outgoing girl called Diana, invited me to join a group of my form-mates in the 'Shrubbery'. 'Tell us all about yourself,' they insisted, with real interest and friendliness - so different from the images my fearful imagination had conjured up from the school stories I had read. In fact, they made quite a heroine of me! As we drew near the end of break, they asked, 'Will you come to Cruse with us on Sunday?'

'What's "Cruse"?' was my puzzled reply.

'Crusaders. It's a sort of Bible class. Come along and bring a Bible and a penny!'

I'd noticed that some of them were wearing those same badges I had seen at my old school, with the four crosses on them, and Diana pointed to hers as she spoke. I was flattered to be asked, but said I would have to ask my mother, for I felt she would not be happy about my getting involved in a 'religious' group. My mother was a person of intellectual integrity, and honestly doubted that there could be a God. She considered it unscholarly to accept what could not be scientifically proved, and queried certain aspects of the Christian faith. She instilled in me a very high regard for intellectual ability and academic achievement.

Aged 17

The Girls' Crusader movement, along with the Boys' which had preceded it by some years, had been founded for young people from private and grammar schools who, for one reason or another, did not attend Sunday Schools attached to the churches. In London I had not been sent to Sunday School, partly because of my mother's attitude to religion, and partly because she felt that the children who went there from the area where we lived were rather 'rough'. When I mentioned the invitation to attend Crusaders, and explained about the movement, she did not raise the same objections as she realised that those who went there were what she described as 'a better class of girl', though she was not too happy about the ideology behind the movement.

After some persistence for some weeks on the part of my new schoolfriends, and especially when I was told that Betty, a near neighbour, had agreed to attend if I did, I finally gave in. Betty and I went along together and sat in the back row, nervously giggling and nudging one another from time to time. Gradually I became impressed by the fact that those leading the class obviously believed what they were teaching. The talks were so different from Scripture lessons at school, where we were taught about historical events that had no impact on our daily lives. At Crusaders Jesus was spoken about as a living person, who knew and loved each of us, had died for us, and wanted to share our lives. His presence was obviously real to those leading the class, and after some months I sensed an inner conviction: this is the truth! Then one afternoon (I was 15 by then) the teaching was based on Christ's invitation in Revelation 3:20: *'Behold, I stand at the door and knock; if anyone hears my voice and opens the door, I will come in....'* I felt Jesus was directly asking me to open my life to him, that he did know me and love me (and I realised I had always felt unknown and unloved) - so I 'opened the door', saying in my heart 'Come in, Lord Jesus,' and I knew that he did. I told no-one about this at the time, but I began to attend the prayer meetings that were held separately and had, in these, a consciousness of the Presence of God in a way that was quite overwhelming. One day I remember it seemed as if the chair against which I was kneeling really shook! I did not join in vocally at these meetings, though I did begin to be conscious of a new self-confidence and easing of my painful shyness in my everyday life.

About a year later I was taken by my oculist, a man who was a very committed Christian, to a series of evangelistic meetings in the Dorking Halls. The main speaker was Captain Reginald Wallis, a well-known 'Plymouth Brother' and father of Arthur Wallis who later became well-known in the early days of the 'charismatic movement'. Years later, when we were both missioners on a UCCF Mission to Exeter University, Arthur told me that he too, as a teenager, had been at those meetings in Dorking! Captain Wallis preached one night on the parable of the Rich Fool in Luke 12, *('This night your soul will be required of you'.)* When he concluded his address with the words, 'Those of you who want to commit your lives wholeheartedly to Christ, look up now and catch my eye as I look around the hall,' I felt my heart thumping as it had done once or twice before when public appeals for commitment were made. I felt a very strong prompting, but hesitated because of the friend sitting beside me who I felt might be critical. Nevertheless, I did look up, and at that moment she did as well! Then Captain Wallis continued, 'Now, will those who have caught my eye now stand up' - which made me feel somehow trapped; but I stood up anyway, and so did my friend. We were asked to go into a side room, and were given some counselling and advice about church attendance and Bible reading and prayer, and given some tracts to take away and read.

This was my first public confession of faith, and it brought me into a closer and deeper fellowship with others in Crusaders. My own sense of assurance of salvation was strengthened, and I began to take my turn at leading the Scripture passage at Crusaders, which involved giving some short comment on it. I found this quite terrifying at first, and felt almost physically sick beforehand! To begin with I did not attend any particular church regularly, but tended to 'shop around'. We lived just opposite Reigate Parish Church - St. Mary Magdalene - but because I was used to the more spontaneous worship and extempore prayer of Crusaders, I found the Anglican liturgy difficult to appreciate. A Choir School was attached to the church and items of choral music seemed to dominate the worship, whereas I felt I wanted to join in and 'be involved' more directly. (Later, St. Mary's became much more open in its worship, and I, in fact, became their CMS Link Missionary while I was in Africa and received great support from them in prayer and in practical ways - they even gave me my first car!) In my teens, however, I settled at the Congregational (now URC) Church, where my friend Betty and her parents attended, joining their choir and tennis club.

Known now as a 'committed' Christian, I began to shape my behaviour to conform to what I understood then was fitting for a Christian. This had repercussions at home - especially when it came to the Cinema. We often went as a family, but I began to feel uncomfortable there as I knew that my Crusader leaders did not go, and that public entertainment of a secular nature was not approved of in evangelical circles then. This was before television brought 'the pictures' into the home - but even that was a long time in gaining acceptance in some Christian circles. So I eventually excused myself from our family trips to the Pictures, to the distress of my mother, who commented, 'I would have thought these new friends of yours would have taught you to be more obedient to your parents!' Leaders at Crusader classes were required to sign a declaration that they would not attend places of public entertainment. This I signed myself when I became a leader some years later. I was teaching at the time, and my lack of knowledge of film-stars used to amaze my pupils, and caused me to begin to query the appropriateness of this extreme 'separation from the world' as we called it, for those who really wanted to communicate the Gospel in contemporary society.

At Crusaders, however, we *were* made aware of the needs of the world, physical as well as spiritual. One of our leaders had worked in Egypt; another had been brought up in China, the daughter of missionaries, and a third went to India as a missionary. Visitors came to speak to us from different parts of the world; we had prayer meetings for specific needs; knitted vests for 'little black babies', and made 'cuff covers' for Chinese people who, apparently, wore them when working to protect their wide flowing sleeves.

At school also, once a term, we had a special visiting speaker. On one occasion, a missionary teacher from Northern Rhodesia (Zambia) gave us a moving picture of her work there among the African girls. She also took a meeting at the Congregational Church in Reigate, and, having been strangely moved by her talk at school, I went along to hear her again. She brought with her a book she had written, called *Children of the Chief*, that I bought and took home to read. In it she told of her early awareness of the need of people in other lands for teachers to share the Gospel with them. 'I'll go one day, dear Lord, if you will have me,' she had prayed. And later God had indeed opened the way for her. Alone in my room I also prayed that prayer. I was 17 ... it was my first conscious call to do something specific with my life, perhaps even overseas. 'Oh, everyone feels like that when they hear a missionary speaker,' said my friends when I told them. But in my heart I felt sure that it was something much more than that.

By this time I was in the 6th form at school, studying for Higher School Certificate (the A levels of those days), and offering History, French, English and RE. Life was very full. I played games enthusiastically, being in the school hockey, cricket and tennis teams. I was, in turn, a House Captain, then Head Girl. These roles gave me experience in handling groups and in public speaking, which was useful preparation for the future. Through these last years at school I did not forget the possibility of the 'mission field'. However, for some time it had been assumed that I would go into teaching (my mother's plan for me), and this meant a university career. So, in my final year, I applied for a Senior County Scholarship as an Education student, had interviews at Westfield College, London, and Bristol University, both of whom offered me a place. I accepted the Bristol offer as Westfield was at that time an all women's college and I felt it would be good to have a change from single-sex education!

So schooldays ended and the summer holidays began. Once again concern about God's way ahead dominated my thinking and praying. Then one evening, as a thunderstorm raged outside, I went to my room, knelt down and prayed earnestly, 'Lord, what is your will for my life?' The answer came, in an audible voice I can never forget: 'I have told you I want you to be a missionary.' For many years I did not tell anyone that I had actually heard a voice, as I felt I would be thought mentally unbalanced! But more recently I have felt free to speak of it, since the charismatic renewal movement has made people more aware of direct manifestations of the Holy Spirit. So convinced was I that God had spoken to me, that I went downstairs and found my father stoking up the boiler for the night. 'Dad, you'll think I'm very foolish to consider throwing away a brilliant career,' I began, 'but I believe I'm meant to be a missionary - so I want to go to Ridgelands Bible College to train, instead of going to the University.' His reply overwhelmed me. 'I don't think you're foolish at all,' he said. 'I believe I was meant to go into the Church, and I didn't do it. If the training you need won't cost more than the university education, I'll support you.' So, Dad was behind me after all! Though Mother, when she heard about it, was most concerned, and even my sister Ruby, when she heard, was angry and tried to dissuade me.

The next day I went to the telephone box at the corner of the road, as I wanted more privacy than I could have on the phone at home, and told my Crusader leader of the decision I had made. As I finished telling her, an amazing joy flooded my heart - a joy I have come to recognise follows acts of obedience and faith. She suggested we meet to talk about it, as we needed to consider carefully the right training for overseas. A professional qualification was necessary for some areas overseas. We agreed to pray for clear guidance whether it would be better for me to go to Bristol and gain a degree and teaching diploma first, before doing specific missionary training. A few days later I received a large envelope from Bristol University, with information about the Hall of Residence and details of the various societies and activities. There was also a notice which said, 'Please fill in and return the enclosed postcard if you are not taking up your place at the University next term' - and there was no postcard in the envelope! To my simple faith at the time, that was my answer!

In September 1938 I went to Bristol to start my university career. My mother was relieved, thinking that I had not got religious mania after all and was now well set on the path she had planned for me.

I started reading for a General Arts degree in History, Latin, French and Economics. In view of my future overseas career I felt a curriculum as wide as possible would be useful. However, after a while I found it rather frustrating not able to go really deeply into any of the subjects, so after discussing this with the professors of the different disciplines, I finally decided on History, and was able to join the Honours course, with Economics as a subsidiary. This proved much more satisfactory to me, though it did lengthen my course by a year, and enabled me to make a special study of Church History, particularly the Reformation period.

The introductory material I had received had included information about BIFCU (Bristol Inter-Faculty Christian Union), who were holding a 'Fresher's Squash' (as informal Christian meetings were often called) on the first Saturday of term. Of course I went along, and heard all about their other meetings and activities. Two of my near neighbours at Manor Hall, my hall of residence, were there too: Marguerite, a 'fresher' like me, and Mary, an Honours Biology student in her final year. Mary asked me what church I attended at home. When I told her I wasn't yet a member of any particular church, she invited me to go with her on Sunday to the Alma Road Chapel, an 'Open Brethren' Assembly, where Professor Rendle-Short, Professor of Surgery at the University, was to be the preacher. Marguerite came with me and we were made very welcome. I felt at home with the religious language and extempore prayers which were much more like those at Crusaders than the more formal liturgies of other churches I had attended. We began going regularly, morning and evening, often being asked to lunch by different members of the congregation. Some time later there was a Believers' Baptism Service, and Mary was one of those being baptised. This service reinforced a concern I had had for some time through my reading of the New Testament, that I had not been baptised in the biblical way. I had seen an old photograph of myself as a baby, dressed in a white lace frock, sitting on a photographer's sofa. Ruby had told me it was taken at my 'christening at St. Gabriel's Church, Pimlico, in the City of Westminster. No-one ever spoke to me about it, except that I knew that an aunt and a cousin of my father's had been godparents, but they did not seem to have any spiritual contact with me. So, on seeing this baptism by immersion, with its deep symbolism, I felt I wanted to be baptised as well 'on my confession of faith'. After much prayer, I approached the 'leading brethren' of the Assembly and asked if they would baptise me on the next occasion. They were very careful in their response, giving quite searching interviews to make sure that I knew the implications of such a step, and that I was truly 'born again'.

The next service was held during a spell of extremely cold weather, when snow was thick on the ground. The water in the baptistry had been heated up to avoid us catching cold, but it proved so very hot that we emerged from it looking like boiled lobsters! Nevertheless, it was a very special occasion. As each of us came up from the water, the congregation sang, 'Be thou faithful unto death, and I will give thee a crown of life.' Then the leading Elder gave us the 'right hand of fellowship' and gave each of us a particular text. I waited with great expectancy for mine, and can still remember the feeling of disappointment when it came: *'Be not weary in well-doing.'* (2 Thessalonians 3:13.) To a 19-year-old it did seem very humdrum and uninspiring. Yet often, through the years, it has proved a challenge not to give up when things became difficult.

Alma Road remained my regular place of worship for much of my time in Bristol, and I have always been grateful for the foundation of solid Bible teaching laid for me by the 'brethren' there throughout those years. But as time went by, one aspect of their practice in particular did cause me some concern, and that was to do with the role, or absence of role, of women in the services, though they did much else of a practical nature, such as catering and flower-arranging. Initially I had noticed that no woman ever led in prayer, made a contribution to the teaching, or even gave out a hymn (except on one occasion when one woman had done so: a silence had ensued until a 'brother' got up and announced a different one!) Sometimes a woman missionary on 'furlough' came and gave a talk to the Women's Meeting in the week, but never at the main Sunday service with men present. Various texts were pointed out to me that at first sight might seem to support this attitude, and I began to be troubled that in BIFCU women did lead meetings, speak and pray in mixed gatherings. Especially this became more and more the case when, in my second year, war broke out and men students (apart from those already enrolled as theological or medical students) were called up before finishing their degrees. Women took even more of a lead, and I found myself elected Missionary Secretary one year, though this did not involve me in any actual public speaking, and for a while I did not even feel free to pray aloud in prayer meetings. In my penultimate year, however, I was asked to stand for President of the Christian Union, and I felt uneasy (as a good 'Plymouth Sister'!) about the public nature of this role. I consulted Professor Rendle-Short about the biblical view concerning this. He reassured me that it was quite appropriate to stand for this office. I did so, and was elected, but not without an initial sense of unease at what seemed an inconsistency of principle between what was biblical in a university meeting but not biblical in the assembly on Sunday.

As a result of the war, King's College, London, had been evacuated to Bristol, and the two Christian Unions merged to form BLIFCU (Bristol and London Inter-Faculty Christian Union), with joint committee. Their president for the year in question, Bill Carlile, and I were joint-presidents, which helped me in my acceptance of the position. Bill was the grandson of Wilson Carlile, the founder of the Church Army, of which Bill himself later became General Secretary. He and other ordinands whom I got to know, as well as other CU members from different denominations, helped me to be less rigid in my outlook, and during my final year especially I began attending and appreciating Anglican and other churches more and more.

Bridesmaid [far left] at Ruby's wedding to Patrick Hubner; Mother and Father second and third on Right

BLIFCU meetings were spiritually upbuilding, and also informative. We had a variety of speakers, many from overseas, who came to help us increase our vision and concern for world evangelisation. One such visitor was Archdeacon Pitt-Pitts, who had just been appointed the first ever Archdeacon of the Anglican Church in Ruanda-Urundi. He shared with us something of the East African Revival, sometimes called the Ruanda Revival though it spread more widely than that. I was puzzled by some of the things he said about it, but that meeting, and his beaming smile, stuck in my mind. I heard, early on, of the IVMF (Inter-Varsity Missionary Fellowship), to join which you were required to make a solemn pledge of willingness to serve God overseas 'if He so willed'. Some time had to elapse between first expressing a desire to join and actually being admitted. Senior BLIFCU members talked with me, pointing out the implications of such a commitment, for example was I prepared for the possibility of remaining single if I embarked on such a calling?

Finally, on 17th April 1940, a small ceremony was held, and I solemnly signed the IVMF membership card. I still have it. The left-hand side reads: 'This declaration is more than a mere expression of willingness or desire to become a Foreign Missionary. It is the statement of a definite life-purpose formed under the direction of God. Those who sign this declaration accept for themselves our Lord's command, "Go ye into all the world, and preach the Gospel to every creature," and dedicate themselves after careful thought and earnest prayer to obey this command, unless prevented by the clear leading of God.' On the right-hand side of the card came the solemn declaration: 'Acknowledging Jesus Christ as my Saviour, my Lord and my God, I purpose, God willing, to serve Him in the Mission Field' - words beneath which my signature now lay. The card was also signed by Farnham St. John, the then Missionary Secretary of the nation-wide Inter-Varsity Fellowship of Evangelical Unions. Farnham himself later became Medical Director of the Christian Hospital in Tangier where I was taken to visit him by his sister, Patricia St. John, the well-known Christian writer and author of the history of the Ruanda Mission, *Breath of Life*. (While she was researching for this in Rwanda, I acted as her interpreter, and she had then invited me to visit her in Morocco.)

The years in Bristol had their stressful times. Bristol suffered many air-raids, during one of which the King's College library was completely lost when an incendiary bomb fell on our Great Hall in which it was being housed. Ironically, their London premises remained unscarred! We were involved in fire-watching, often from the room at the top of the University Tower, from where we would climb out on to the sloping roofs, searching for incendiaries after a raid. From time to time we would hear news of former fellow-students reported missing or killed, and the realisation of what lay ahead for so many cast an air of seriousness over what are normally carefree days. We did have our times of fun, however, including 'rags', such as the time when Winston Churchill, our University Chancellor, came for Convocation. A group of students 'captured' the Lord Mayor's coach in which he was travelling, diverted it to the Student Union building, and made an amusing address to him - a prank he played along with good-humouredly! Sports continued too, though in the later years of the war travelling was limited. I played hockey for the Women's 1st Eleven and we won the Women's Inter-Varsity Hockey Cup. We played Manchester in the finals, at Birmingham, and as we paraded the trophy through the streets to the station, there were cries of, 'Ee! They've wun a cuup!' The Vice-Chancellor invited us all to a sherry party, but several of us were members of the Christian Union so politely asked for 'soft drinks'. One year I took up rowing and was included in the Women's Eight, and sometimes I was called on to play for the University in mixed tennis doubles.

After graduating, I joined the Education Department to obtain a Diploma in Education, after which I was obliged to teach for at least two years. In any case, I would have been called up into the forces unless I had done this. So, in 1943, I joined the staff of the Raine Foundation School (a Church of England foundation), evacuated from Stepney to Hurstpier point in Sussex. I taught History, RE and PE, especially games. As it was an 'East End' school, quite a percentage of the girls were Jewish and proved most able students. I enjoyed being in Sussex, so near the sea, which, although it was in the restricted coastal area, we could visit - as we were already within the restricted zone! My billet was most pleasant, being with a hospitable family in the village, where the husband was gardener on a big nearby estate and brought home vegetables and fruit. A land-girl also shared the billet, which gave me an insight into that kind of life also. It was not entirely a quiet retreat as we had many flying bombs over us, some of which fell before reaching their London targets.

My sense of vocation to overseas mission did not leave me, and when the war ended and I could be released from my contract to teach in England, I began to pray earnestly about where this should be, for as yet I had no clear guidance. My first interest had been Japan, and then, through my reading of Amy Carmichael, South India, particularly Dohnavur, where she had founded her community for girls rescued from temple prostitution. Later, Africa started to draw me again, as it had when the missionary speaker at school had occasioned my first commitment. Having had some contact with the General Secretary of the then Africa Inland Mission, I sent for application papers, but, strangely, every time I picked up my pen to begin on the form, my hand seemed so heavy I felt I could hardly start writing.

During the Easter holidays, 1945, I attended a conference for teachers of RE which was being held in Oxford and organised by the Inter-Varsity Fellowship of Evangelical Unions' Graduates Fellowship. Just before leaving home I met the vicar of Holy Trinity Church, Redhill (where I had started attending during the school holidays), the Revd. Hugh Evan-Hopkins. His father had been one of the founders of the Keswick Convention, and Hugh himself had recently returned from service as a missionary at Dohnavur. He had also done some travelling around the University for IVF and I had met him at BIFCU and told him about my sense of 'call'. 'Doreen,' he said, 'if you don't take some steps very soon towards going overseas, you'll find you've settled down in England and never actually go.' 'But the Lord hasn't shown me yet where he wants me,' I replied. 'What about Ruanda?' he asked (he was a member of the Ruanda Council at that time). 'But it's a *medical* mission, 'I answered, knowing its title to be the Ruanda General and Medical Mission, CMS - and that their pioneer missionaries had been doctors. 'Yes,' he answered, 'but they are wanting to develop educational work and are looking for teachers.' At the time I brushed off this remark and set off for Oxford.

On arriving I discovered that the hosts of the conference were Dr. Algernon and Mrs. Zoë Stanley-Smith who, together with her brother Dr. Leonard Sharp and his wife, had been the pioneers of the Ruanda Mission! During the first day I met several people whom I knew. Two of them, quite separately, asked me where I was teaching, and when I said Hurstpierpoint they each told me there was a prayer meeting held in the next village run by a Ruanda missionary on leave. Some others I talked to brought up the subject of Ruanda, and I felt as though I was being bombarded by the name of this country whose geographical location I hardly knew.

Lunch took place in the various city colleges and that day I was allocated to St. Hilda's. Waiting in the bus queue, I realised I was standing next to Mrs. Stanley-Smith! I can still recall my beating heart, and thinking 'I can't just say to someone I've not met that I'm wondering if I'm being called to Ruanda.' So I kept quiet and got on the bus. There was only one vacant seat - next to Mrs. Stanley-Smith! After a few moments I heard myself saying as casually as I could, 'I was interested to hear of your ministry in Ruanda, and would like to hear more about it.' 'Come to coffee in our room after lunch and meet my husband,' she replied straightaway. This I duly did, and was greeted by 'Dr. Algie', as he was always known, coming in rubbing his hands and announcing, 'This is wonderful! At our Council meeting we have just decided to ask the Lord for ten educationalists in the next ten years - and you're the first!' 'But Miss Peck is only enquiring, dear,' his wife interjected, but he continued undaunted, showing me photographs and leaflets of the country and outlining something of their plans to develop teacher-training colleges and expand their school work. One leaflet in particular caught my eye. It began, 'Ruanda is the Switzerland of Africa - a land of hills and valleys.'

After coffee, as we returned to the conference hall for the afternoon session, and feeling I was being swept along by his enthusiasm, I made a definite prayer that God would give me a very specific confirmation, from the Bible, if it was indeed his will that I pursue the possibility of Ruanda further. I felt that something more was needed on which to base a life's work than chance encounters with people and a meeting in a bus queue!

The first speaker that afternoon was Lucy Nelson, a doctor who had been working on the north-west frontier of India, waiting for the opportunity to enter Nepal, where she believed that God had called her. Nepal was at that time completely closed to Christian work; nevertheless, so clear did she feel God's call to her had been, that she was sure the door would open for her. As she began to speak, she pointed down the hall, seemingly straight at me, and, quoting Deuteronomy 11:11 said, *'The land whither thou goest is a land of hills and valleys...'* A voice in my heart said, 'the Switzerland of Africa!' This verse had been given to Dr. Lucy Nelson as part of the confirmation of her call, as Nepal is also, of course, a land of hills and valleys, but I knew the Lord had led her to share it then, especially for me. When the session ended I went straight up to Dr. Stanley-Smith and told him, 'For my part I feel I should ask your Council to consider my offer for service with the Ruanda Mission, and trust that interviews, medicals, etc., will make clear what is the Lord's will.' To my amazement he replied, 'I have just received a cheque for £200 to pay for a missionary's passage. I consider that is a seal on your call!'

After the conference I went home to Reigate. My mother was there and asked if I'd had an interesting time, then went on to tell me of a meeting she'd had with an old neighbour of ours whose son I had played with when we were children. 'Douglas has gone off to work in South

Africa,' she said, 'Why don't you go abroad? If I had my time over again I wouldn't just stay in England!' When I replied that I was indeed considering this, she was initially very pleased, though not so enthusiastic when I explained that it would be as a missionary. However, telling her of my plans had turned out to be easier than I had imagined!

The application forms that I received from the Ruanda Mission of CMS seemed almost to fill themselves in - so different from my experience with previous application forms! There was, however, one matter that caused me some disquiet and that was that I discovered I would be required to attend the CMS Training College, still evacuated to Ridley Hall, Cambridge. Though I had no first-hand knowledge, I had gained an impression that it was somewhat 'liberal' in its theology. I therefore mentioned on my application form that I was not happy at the prospect of training there. Naturally, in the various interviews I was given, some interviewers raised this question with me. In fact, I was even asked to talk to Dr. Max Warren, the then General Secretary of CMS, about it. Then Ena Price, the Women's Secretary, challenged me to kneel down and tell the Lord what I really knew first-hand about the content of the training course and the biblical standpoint of the College, and then make my decision. Of course I knew nothing!

So I waited for the next indication of the Lord's leading. When I received a letter from CMS accepting me 'as a CMS missionary for service with the Ruanda Mission' and *inviting* me to join their main CMS candidates in training, I was humbled and amazed - humbled at the graciousness of the CMS leaders in inviting me to join their training college, which I had presumed to criticise, and amazed that they had actually accepted me as a missionary when others were accepted as 'candidates in training'. Consequently, sensing God's directing hand, I resigned my teaching post and set out for Ridley Hall in September 1945.

The autumn term in Cambridge was a most enjoyable and stimulating time. As well as joining in many of the Ridley Hall lectures for ordinands, there were other interesting public lectures in the town - particularly I remember a series of theological lectures by Bishop Stephen Neill - and we had the opportunity to join with the male ordinands in ward services in Addenbrooke's Hospital. We ate in the Ridley Hall dining room, though at the opposite end of the room from the men! Traditionally women had not been allowed to eat in men's colleges in Cambridge, so history had been made when a special dispensation of the University Senate allowed the CMS women students to eat there. At that time when men were only just beginning to be demobbed from the forces, we women outnumbered the ordinands, of whom there were only six! One of these later became a pioneer Anglican missionary in the Congo, and another was John Stott, later to become an internationally respected teacher and preacher.

In January 1946 Foxbury, the CMS Women's Training College in Chislehurst, Kent, was vacated by the ATS who had been billeted there during the war, and we began the process of moving back from Cambridge. Most of our free time during the first term was spent thoroughly cleaning the place, rehanging curtains and tidying up the gardens. One day I was told I was too much of an academic and could only think at the end of a pencil! This remark was sparked off by the excuse I had given, when ill-prepared for a seminar, that I had been too busy scraping the bathroom walls of the rather obscene posters that the ATS had stuck there. 'Overseas, you will have to prepare talks, etc., while doing practical things,' I was informed, and to give me practice in this I was sent to work on the farm at the St. Julian's Community in Sussex during the spring holiday. I gathered mangel-wurzels from a heap into a wheelbarrow and trundled them along to feed the pigs; cleaned out cow-sheds; fed calves separated from their mothers; and generally rejoiced in the countryside, fresh air and farm life. Little had it been realised how much I would be in my element! One day, Miss Florence Allshorn, the leader and founder of the community, and former principal of the CMS Women's Training College, asked me, 'Are you getting what you came for?' 'I'm not sure,' I replied, 'I believe I'm supposed to be learning to meditate.' 'Try making up poetry,' she advised. So, as I trundled my wheelbarrow along I tried, 'The sky is blue, the trees are green....' but the muse did not inspire me! However, as I talked with others who were there, especially Miss Irene Tatham, who later became Vice-Principal at Foxbury, and as I read books at the silent meal-times, I began to appreciate an aspect of spirituality of which I had no previous experience - contemplative prayer and meditation.

The time at St. Julian's was the beginning of an increasing acceptance that God speaks to people in different ways, and that Christians from traditions and backgrounds other than my conservative evangelical one could be truly born of the Spirit of God, and had fresh insights to share that enriched one's understanding of the 'whole counsel of God', and his activity in the world. Florence Allshorn, who visited us at Foxbury from time to time, provided an illustration of this different approach. In one of her seminars she said, 'The present generation has forgotten how to *look*, to really *look*, and learn not just with the mind but through the senses and let what they see speak to them.' She sent us off to different parts of the grounds to do just that. I spent the time gazing at a clump of aubretia, absorbing the differences of colour and the blending of the many shades on the tiny florets which together made up that blaze of glory.

Throughout the years I have often looked back with gratitude to the training I received at the CMS College, where there was such a forward-looking vision of what the expatriate's contribution should be in other cultures. CMS realised that culture was important, and it wasn't the job of the missionary to anglicise it. Christ could enter into every culture, the Holy Spirit expressing Christianity in a way that was right and appropriate for each country. This has been one of the great contributions of CMS to world mission - and I was grateful for their breadth of vision, and for their ability to follow the Spirit's leading, rather than hardening into traditional patterns of work and witness.

During the Easter holidays I was sent to a parish in inner Manchester for 'work experience', joining in the various meetings, services and visiting with which the church was involved. It was an added bonus to be sharing this experience with Gladys Shaw who later served for many years in the Aurangabad area of Central India, and whom I had the joy of visiting there many years later. She wrote two informative, amusing and inspiring books, We *Came to a Village* and *I Lived in a Village*, and on my visit to her she took me to several of these villages, involving me in evangelistic village work. But in Manchester we were put together to help and challenge each other, and report on our reactions and progress.

For further practical, non-bookish experience I was sent for three weeks to Bristol Maternity Hospital - a difficult assignment for me as I had an irrational fear of hospitals, and was not used to babies. Witnessing births, changing endless nappies and learning to bath new-borns did stand me in very good stead in Africa, when I often had to interpret for new medics in hospitals or clinics, or got involved in emergency births in strange places!

As I was now well set on my preparation for a missionary career in Africa, and beginning the process of packing and getting ready to sail, my mother became much more reconciled to the prospect, and began to take an interest in my future work once she understood it would involve running schools and training teachers, not just imitating a Sunday School picture of standing under a palm tree holding up pictures to the locals. She even began holding coffee mornings for people to meet me and learn about what I was going to do, feeling not a little proud, I suspect, that I was launching out in this way. She was encouraged too by meeting some of the other mission workers - doctors, teachers, clergymen - on home leave, and finding them academically well qualified and intelligent people. But one thing she was very adamant about, and that was that I should not conform to stereotype in dress and appearance. 'If you *must* be a missionary, at least need you *look* like one? Your hair looks dreadful, why don't you have a perm? Is finance a problem? - Here's five quid!' - enough to have my long straight hair transformed into short permanent waves. As I was packing my heavy luggage to go in advance, she would ask, 'Have you got enough cutlery? You know I've got all Gran's as well, so do take anything you need.' And, 'You know I don't care for dress-making - would you like to take Gran's sewing machine?' (a very nice Singer). It was hard to pack but it served me well for many years, and on finally leaving Africa, a pastor's wife received it with great joy.

So relationships were good as the time for departure drew near, and both my parents drove me down to Southampton for the ship.

Chapter 2
Journey to Rwanda

I sailed from Southampton on the *Winchester Castle* on the 18th December 1946. The ship had not yet been refitted after being used as a troop ship, so we women were eight to a cabin. I found myself in the same cabin as two other CMS missionaries, Miss Lang of Kumi Leprosy Settlement (later to receive the OBE) and Miss Langley, a teacher in Uganda. Among the other passengers were a CMS couple working in Kenya; a Church of Scotland minister, Jack Wilkinson, going to Karatina in Kenya; a BMS widow and her young son, going back to the Congo; and Margaret Syson, another Ruanda Mission recruit, whose husband was waiting for her in Kenya, having been discharged from the Army there. At the first opportunity I wrote to my parents, describing in detail my first days on board ship:

'We set sail at 2 p.m. yesterday and went on deck to see the tugs getting us out into Southampton Water. Then we went slowly down till nearly opposite Cowes, then turned ... and went straight towards Spithead. It was getting dark by then, so we couldn't see the Island very clearly, but we could make out Ryde and the headlands towards Sandown... We had a muster on deck at 4.30 and then went below.

The boat is very crowded and at night there is very little space to sit. I think bed is the best place and then try to get up early. The men are very badly off as they are in a huge dormitory of 120 with little cupboard or drawer space, and only two baths! Everyone is very annoyed about it and say that during the War things were much better. The food, though, is very good and plenty of it - bread, butter, eggs, sugar, cakes in abundance and four-course dinners.' (Rationing was still in force in England when I left.) 'In the Shop there are almost forgotten luxuries - silk stockings, chocolate, watches, handbags, tennis shoes, films, fountain pens - in fact, there seems to be no end to all the amazing things they have packed away. Cigarettes are next to nothing and the ration is 200 a week. Believe it or not, the Bay of Biscay is as calm as a millpond and the sun has been streaming down. Apparently we shall be in Port Said for Christmas as she is going very quickly. She is a fine-looking boat and apparently is steadier than the Queen Elizabeth.'

Two days later - 'we sighted Africa today. Range beyond range of curious-shaped mountains and on the other side - Spain, with white villages nestling at the foot of towering limestone escarpments. Then on through the Straits and past the famous Rock (Gibraltar). The straits are far wider than I'd imagined - about 7 miles. The sun has been brilliant all day and we've been on deck, sitting on chairs on the top deck in fact. The sea is even more smooth than ever and so beautifully blue.'

The sea journey took 18 days and we had plenty of time to get to know one another, as well as acclimatise ourselves and adjust to the prospect of a different culture. A group of us met together for Bible studies and held activities, with a Christian content, for the children. On Christmas Day we found ourselves steaming towards Port Said; festivities were organised and we had a splendid Christmas dinner. After Christmas it began to get very hot; my summer clothes were in my trunk which had been placed in the hold by mistake, so I had to borrow something cooler from my friends. The Chief Steward said he would go down and look for it when we docked at Port Said. Eventually, he emerged looking very hot and somewhat cross, having taken a long time searching, and announced, 'It's not a trunk, it's a suitcase! The definition of a trunk is handles at both ends. Yours has only one handle, in the middle!' I was duly apologetic, and to my astonishment he turned to a fellow officer and commented, 'It's hard to be

In Port Said [far right]

cross with her, she has such a charming manner!' This was completely unconscious on my part as I had never thought before about the impression I might be making, and had certainly never had such a remark before!

'We were able to go ashore at Port Said,' I wrote home in my letter, 'and spent the whole day there. As soon as the ship drew towards the quayside, she was surrounded by dozens of little boats full of Arabs selling leather goods of all kinds such as handbags, zip holdalls, suitcases, pouches, etc. Very nice though not really very cheap - at least not to begin with, for those experienced in the art of bargaining managed to get hold of some things quite reasonably. It was strange to watch it all. First the men would hold up an article and shout out in broken English how good it was, and the price, then the would-be purchaser suggested a lower one, and so it went on till the bargain was struck. Next a rope was thrown up and the article was hauled up, plus a bag for the return of the cash. This went on all day, right up till the last minute before we finally sailed again. One of the big shops in Port Said sent some goods on board and set up a shop there. Simon Artz is the name. We went to this shop when we got ashore and found it full of all kind of things we'd not seen for years, but they were all very expensive. I bought a few postcards and a little brass tray, but otherwise was content to admire from the other side of the counter.

'We only went through the main streets and didn't see much of the city except the water front, for apparently there is a great deal of anti-British feeling about and we were warned to do nothing to aggravate international bad feeling. We had lunch in a very impressive-looking hotel with a well-laid out tropical garden at the rear. It was all extremely nice and well served.... There were masses of fruit everywhere, of course, and some rather lovely purple flowering shrubs, but the place itself was dusty and the children particularly were very grubby. We were continuously surrounded by street sellers offering all kinds of goods: perfumes, jewellery, etc., and I succumbed to having my photo taken! Margaret Syson who is coming to Ruanda is standing next to me.

'It was dark by the time we went through the Suez canal,' I continued, 'so it was rather difficult to get an idea of what it was like, though we could make out vague shapes on the land, and were just in time to see the end of it at dawn, and the colouring was really lovely. Then we passed out into the Red Sea, which didn't look a bit red and is far wider than I'd thought, for we didn't see land on either side for nearly two days. There has been a delightful breeze all the time, so it hasn't been at all hot - for the Red Sea, that is! - though, of course, the sun is very strong.'

Going through the Gulf of Suez was fascinating, as we had our first sight of the desert, and trains of camels plodding steadily along with their loads. At Port Suez the 'Gilly-gilly' man came aboard with his sleight-of-hand tricks with chickens, and as we steamed further down, what was reputed to be Mount Sinai was pointed out to us in the distance. At Port Sudan we went out in a glass-bottomed boat over the coral reef, and saw multitudes of brightly coloured tropical fish and corals. There was time for a walk along the coast where we picked up sponges and pieces of coral. Returning to the ship we found 'Fuzzy-wuzzies' (as they used to be called) of the Sudan loading the ship, and reacting angrily when people tried to photograph them. This was when I had my first experience of the superior attitude towards Africans of some of the white South African passengers. In fact as I witnessed their unspeakably discourteous behaviour, I felt ashamed to be white.

We reached Aden just as the sun was setting and it was a most impressive sight. 'There are rugged cliffs surrounding the harbour,' I wrote, 'and the town itself is built five miles inland. We went ashore in motorboats and then took a car to the town. It was lovely to swish along in the moonlight up the steep hillside, through the rock at the top, and down again to the hubbub of the Arabs' talk. I've never seen such a crowded street - people, goats and cows, wandering about or standing at the shop doorways where all kinds of food and drink were being sold. There were lots of lovely materials too, but they are subject to Customs, so I thought it better to wait until we get to Uganda. Fruit was ridiculously dear, though, for they seemed to think we'd had none in England and would pay any price. It all seemed so strange and remote, as though one were watching a picture and yet were part of it!' Mingling in the crowds coming up from the market I had a strange sense of heaviness of spirit, that I later came to recognise as the oppression resulting from demonic activity.

We sailed down the coast of Africa, and I slept on deck because it was so hot and balmy. Crossing the Equator, I was puzzled to see the constellations the wrong way up, then realised that was because we were in the Southern hemisphere! I was delighted by my first sight of the Southern Cross.

During the voyage it was borne in on me that the term 'Ruanda Revival' conjured up in some Christians' minds a picture of people with a 'holier than thou' attitude. Some of the missionaries on board who had worked in Uganda explained that they had felt that any spiritual experience of theirs was discounted by the 'Revival brethren', because they did not use the same religious terminology. 'Dr. Joe Church would think I'm not saved,' said one, while others seemed to expect of me a very high standard of faith and practice. So far I had, personally, had little first-hand experience of the 'Way of Revival', with its emphasis on 'Walking in the Light' and 'Testimony to the Power of the Blood of Jesus to break the power of repented sin' - though having had a definite conversion experience I was able to understand these terms, and had also found the Ruanda missionaries whom I'd met in England to be of the same theological background as my Crusader and University Christian Union friends. Earlier, at a CMS conference in England, one missionary teacher from Uganda had warned me to avoid the 'balokole' (Luganda for 'saved ones' and used widely for those in the Revival movement), sharing her own experience of them in Uganda. She deplored what she felt was their presumption in appearing to judge the spiritual state of others. 'Some even say the bishop isn't saved!' she had said, adding, 'I don't think anyone should say that about another; in fact, I don't think anyone can assert that they themselves are saved.' I remember being troubled by this last remark, feeling strongly that a Christian should have that assurance, and was disturbed that someone so unsure of her salvation could have been accepted and sent out as a missionary. (A year later I met this same person again in Uganda where I'd gone on a short holiday. She greeted me with a hug, and the words, 'Praise the Lord, Doreen, I've been saved! I'm so glad what I said to you in England didn't stop you having fellowship with the Revival brethren!')

On the voyage, though, I still knew little of the controversies arising from the Revival. I was feeling somewhat cautious, nevertheless I was so sure God had called me to work in Ruanda that I assumed I would automatically be part of what the Holy Spirit was doing in the Church.

We docked at Mombasa on the 4th January 1947. It was very hot. In the Customs shed I was met by Peter and Elisabeth Guillebaud on their way back to England with their young family, John, David and Margaret. (Meg, now ordained, returned to Rwanda in 1995 to train pastors, and was joined by her mother after Peter's death.) Peter and Elisabeth had been the first qualified educationalists in Ruanda. After a break in England to see their children through their training, they returned to launch the work of the Scripture Union in Ruanda, going back again, in their seventies, to oversee the completion of the new translation of the Bible into Kinyarwanda.

I had never met them before and we only had time for a very quick word together before they had to go on board ship, for their first furlough in eight years, the War having prevented them taking home leave before. Little did I know then how closely we were to work together in subsequent years. I recall standing there with all my luggage around me in that Customs shed, marvelling that I really was there, in Africa - I who seemed a most unlikely 'foreign missionary', growing up in the back streets of Westminster, with no early Christian upbringing, and painfully shy! But now I had to face the practicalities of the journey. Our heavy luggage was put 'in bond' for Ruanda; but I had heard that Joy Gerson had done this, and had only just received it after five months. I discovered it was possible to take it with you and reclaim the duty if it was officially sealed and the seal unbroken at the other end. 'This was where the fun began,' I wrote to my parents, 'for I had eight packages of various shapes and sizes which had to be wound round with pieces of wire. It took ages and now I have heart attacks when the packages are thrown around, that these seals will be ripped off! I was most fortunate with the Customs officials that I had to deal with, for they vary such a lot. They were most helpful and polite in every way and even struck off many of the taxable things and called them "second-hand"!'

The train journey to Kampala was quite an experience, as in those days the accommodation was extremely comfortable. 'Kanzu' (a long white cotton garment) clad waiters served sumptuous meals in the restaurant car, and other officials of East African Railways prepared our bunks for the night. At stations on the journey up country, people came to the train windows to sell us drinks and fruit. We reached Nairobi at noon and left the train to drive out for the night to some cousins of Margaret Syson's who were coffee planters. The Steeles lived on a lovely estate, cool and beautiful, surrounded by wide green lawns and exotic flowerbeds. 'We had chicken, green peas, new potatoes and sprouts with Christmas pudding and cream for dinner, besides masses of fruit and cool drinks,' I wrote to my mother. 'I saw how the coffee is separated, washed and dried before going to the mills for roasting; it was most interesting.... Every kind of vegetable seems to grow at the same time here, along with pineapples, passion-fruit and bananas, and the flower garden is a blaze of colour.' I was interested to meet some Kikuyu people after hearing so much about them and reading of them in Jomo Kenyatta's book *Facing Mount Kenya*. He had returned to Kenya a few months earlier after years in exile and there was a spirit of euphoria among the Kikuyu at the expectation of what his leadership would mean for Kenya and their tribe.

Next day we caught the train again and thrilled with the spectacular scenery as we climbed the escarpment and looked down the Great Rift Valley towards Mount Kilimanjaro - an unbelievable experience for me in those days before television programmes made such views more familiar.

Another night on the train. Then - Uganda! Bananas everywhere! (We'd had none in England since before the War.) I had a table in my compartment, so for almost the first time was able to write a legible letter home describing how it felt to be in Africa at last. 'It is strange how normal everything seems - even to see oranges and pineapples growing, and the most glorious coloured trees and flowers, and to eat mangoes and bananas ad-lib.... You would love the flowers, Mother - all the English ones out together, besides the brilliant cannas, amaryllis, bougainvillaea and frangipani, and many others I don't know the names of.'

At Mukono station a crowd of missionaries from the Theological College were waiting on the platform to welcome us, led by John V. Taylor (later to become CMS General Secretary and subsequently Bishop of Winchester). One of his challenging books, *The Primal Vision*, discusses the concepts of God which are present among people completely untouched by Christian evangelism or education. Quite early on I had my first experience of this when I met a Pygmy lady who had named her little girl Uwimana Ndayisenga, meaning 'The one from God to whom I pray'. We very much appreciated the custom of the Mukono missionaries of coming down to greet those going further up country; it was good to be thus welcomed. We then went on to Kampala itself, where the railway virtually ended, arriving on the 8th January 1947. We'd been two days and nights on the train.

In Kampala we were met and driven up to the CMS centre on Namirembe Hill ('the Hill of Peace') on which stands the Anglican Cathedral (where Alexander Mackay, the great pioneer to Uganda, is buried) and Mengo Hospital, a famous Mission hospital for many years, but now a Government one. I was taken to stay with a CMS couple, Dr. Roy and Mrs. Dora Billington, who made me very welcome indeed. Roy was Medical Superintendent of Mengo Hospital and later in the week he took me round the hospital. I found it much easier than I feared, for the usual sinking feeling I always experienced in English hospitals with their clinical atmosphere was absent and everything was so relaxed. Among the patients, who were all very welcoming, was a delightful Tutsi lady -

my first contact with a Munyarwanda. She tried to teach me some vocabulary! Dora, in her turn, whizzed me round Kampala, and to various meetings and groups. One ordeal I remember vividly was her delegating me to test some Girl Guides for their Badge in Knots. My knowledge of 'Sheepshank' and 'Clove-hitch' was decidedly shaky, though I could tell a 'Granny'. I think I passed them all, as they all seemed so confident! It was my first 'all on my own' contact with African girls, and I can still feel the excitement and yet the strangeness of it.

Roy and Dora were right in the heart of the Revival, and I was at once aware of the deep fellowship which this movement of the Holy Spirit had engendered. Africans were in and out of the house, and I warmed to the openness and obvious recognition of the Lord's presence at all times. On my first evening they held a New Year Party at which I was able to meet many people, though I had to borrow a dress because my main luggage was still 'in bond' and I hadn't kept with me anything 'posh' enough for such an occasion. Two visitors came in specifically to talk to me. One called William. The name William Nagenda meant nothing to me then, but I have never forgotten his words in greeting: 'We are always delighted to welcome new missionaries who know the Lord Jesus Christ as their personal Saviour, and who will throw themselves into the Revival from the start.' I felt awkward and insecure, and supposed he was doubting my openness to revival. Meeting him later in the year, and having become more sure of my sympathy with revival, I confessed to him my reaction at our first meeting. 'Oh no!' he said at once, 'We had heard that you were saved and open to fellowship and were genuinely delighted to welcome you!' I realised then how easily remarks by the 'brethren' (as the Revival leaders were known) could be misunderstood and taken as questioning the spiritual status of even long-serving missionaries. For me, though, this was the beginning of many years of fellowship and deepening friendship with both William (a highly educated Ugandan and one time Headmaster of Gahini Boys' School) and his wife Sara, one that lasted until his death in 1973. However, I did feel uncomfortable at first at 'fellowship' meetings - not quite part of what was going on, though outwardly I went along with the singing and rejoicing.

The singing of the 'balokole' ('saved ones') was certainly carried on with great joy and spontaneity. They shared with each other any failures they'd had since their last meeting (usually daily) and asked forgiveness from those involved and from God. After each testimony they would sing a song of praise, 'Tukutendereza Yesu' ('We praise you, Jesus'), continuing with a rather free translation of the chorus: 'Glory, glory,

Halleluyah! Glory, glory to the Lamb! Oh, the cleansing Blood has reached me - Glory, glory to the Lamb' from the old hymn 'Precious Jesus Thou hast saved me.' This chorus had become the signature tune of the Revival throughout East Africa. The word 'Tukutendereza' was widely used as a greeting among Christians. Wherever you met them, in the market, the Government offices, or at the Post Office, you would be greeted by it. Some of the Europeans felt there was rather too much repetition of the singing of this chorus, but it was sung because the 'balokole' genuinely felt the wonder of the Lord's saving grace and responded spontaneously when they heard testimonies about this.

Later in my first week in Uganda I was taken by Roy Billington to meet Simeon Nsibambi, William Nagenda's brother-in-law, and a former Government official. Along with Dr. Joe Church, he was used as a channel of the Holy Spirit in the early days of the Revival. Simeon came from a wealthy family but had given up all social and material advantages to go round preaching the Gospel. As he and Joe Church had 'searched the Scriptures' together for the key to the outpouring of the Spirit for which they both longed, they discovered how closely this outpouring was linked to repentance and the acceptance by faith of the efficacy of the Precious Blood of Jesus to cleanse repented sin. Simeon always liked to give a special 'word' to new people and to discover their spiritual experience. As I entered the room, 'Are you saved?' he enquired straightaway. 'Yes, praise the Lord, I am,' I promptly replied. 'Since when?' .... And the catechising continued.

We then shared our experiences more deeply, and after a while he turned to the Bible and read out to me Ephesians 3:16f: *'That he would grant you, according to the riches of his glory, to be strengthened with might by his Spirit in the inner man; that Christ may dwell in your hearts by faith.'* Although I knew this verse by heart, and was sure of being 'saved', it was to be some years before I began consciously to experience the reality spoken of in these verses.

It was on Sunday, 12th January 1947, that I attended my first church service in Africa. We went to the Namirembe Cathedral for the 7 a.m. Communion, which was in English. Afterwards I was taken to see the grave with the single name 'Mackay' on the simple cross. What an amazing spiritual transformation had come about by God's grace in the sixty years since he had arrived in Africa!

The next day I met the Bishop of Uganda, Cyril Stuart, and his wife Mary for the first time. They offered to help me on my journey by giving me a lift from Kabale (where the Bishop was to hold a Confirmation service) to Buye, in northern Urundi, where they were due to attend the Diocesan Conference. (At this time the Diocese of Uganda included Ruanda-Urundi as well.) It was considered 'a good thing' for me to go to Buye too, to meet 'the Church' as it were.

So on the 15th January I set off from Kampala with Stanley and Margaret Syson on the first leg of my journey by road to Ruanda, down the one long road to Kabale, near the Ruanda/Uganda border. Stanley and Margaret had squeezed me into their not-too-reliable car, packed to the roof, and with an African passenger almost buried beneath all the luggage! We spent the night in the Ankole Hotel at Mbarara. The hotel was pleasant, though not over-plentiful with food! I was amused to see the towels were stamped with the words "Stolen from the Ankole Hotel"!

Next day we pushed on over treacherous dirt roads and had puncture and gear trouble. We also had a continuously changing audience of curious onlookers when we stopped for our picnic lunch. Then we proceeded more quickly as the roads became drier over the last lap of the journey. The countryside grew more and more beautiful as we went west. We called in for a brief visit at Kisiizi, where there was a Mission hospital, and climbed the hill to the Mission compound at Kabale. Finally we paid a flying visit to the shore of Lake Bunyoni (whose name means 'Lake of Little Birds'), though a broken spring on the car prevented our going across to Bwama, the island where the leprosy settlement was situated. It was so beautiful in the deepening evening shadows, and the singing of two men paddling their canoe across the lake took us right out of the bustle of 20th century civilisation.

The Kabale area was one of the loveliest places I had ever seen. 'It has deep valleys and rolling hills, and nearby the most wonderful lake dotted with islands. Kabale itself is over 6,000 feet high, so quite cool, and with flowers growing in abundance. There are masses of sweet peas, violets, hollyhocks, roses, lupins, dahlias, gladioli, sunflowers - in fact, there's no end to the list,' I wrote. I stayed a few days with Miss Constance Hornby, who was Head of the Girls' School in Kabale. She became quite a legend in Uganda during her many years of service there - and had a swamp (Hornby Swamp) named after her! I spent some time visiting the Kabale Preparatory School, a school originally established by the Ruanda Mission for the children of missionaries and Government officials. The English staff were members of the Ruanda Mission CMS so they were my first contact with the Ruanda Mission in Africa. The school was high up on the hill; from it could be seen the volcanoes of the Bufumbira Mountain range, 8,000 to 16,000 feet high, which form the Uganda/Congo/Ruanda border, and are the home of the great mountain gorilla. The air was cool and beautiful.

My first morning I was given breakfast in bed, and then had a chance to explore the Kabale mission compound and meet some Ruandan girls, who tried to teach me a few words of their language. There had been much singing going on late into the night - I heard the chorus 'Tukutendereza' again and again. Miss Hornby apologised for the disturbance, and I, to my shame now, remember saying rather patronisingly, 'It's the effervescence of spiritual adolescence I suppose.' The following day I met Dr. Godfrey Talbot-Hindley, one of the leaders of the mission in Ruanda. He and his wife Phyllis were to be my 'senior missionaries' later on. Around the church (later to become the Cathedral) at Kabale, people were singing as they gathered for the Confirmation service being held the next day.

On the Sunday morning over 700 people were confirmed by Bishop Stuart, and over 1,000 took Communion. Thousands thronged outside the church too. In the afternoon there was Evensong in English, to which some Government officials came, and Bishop Stuart preached on 'Following the Star', using a rather unusual story of three people who went to the Stable, an Indian, an African and a European, who, entering the stable separately first, found not a baby but someone like themselves. Then they went in together and found the baby! The Sysons came to supper, we had some singing, and four African visitors came in to talk with us all.

We set off on Monday morning quite early for a visit to Lake Bunyoni, but were delayed by sticking gears as usual, so arrived at the lakeside later than planned. The day was just perfect as we were rowed across the calm waters amid patches of beautiful blue water lilies, to the rhythmic swing of the rowers. On reaching the Leprosy island, Bwama, Dr. Leonard Sharp took us round the hospital, and explained to us the two different types of leprosy. We also met people in various stages of the disease. Then we visited the church and climbing the tower, had a marvellous view of the whole island. Dinner was at the Nurses' House (shared by Janet Metcalf and Marguerite Barley, whom I'd first met at the CMS Training College in Chislehurst, and a teacher, Grace Mash), then we were given another lake trip to 'Sharp's Island' to meet Mrs. Esther Sharp. The island sat like a green gem on the blue water of the lake, and the gardens were beautiful, though at first sight (so I wrote in my diary) perhaps a little too like Henley! We had a good swim, finding the water very cold, and had tea on the island. Dr. Len Sharp then took us all back in his motorboat to the mainland. Back in Kabale packing had to be hurried through, then there was fellowship together and we found much to talk about. I was surprised that the sight of the disfigurements of the leprosy patients had not upset me as I had imagined beforehand that it would; and I still remember the radiance in the scarred, blind face of one of the many patients who were so obviously full of love for the Lord Jesus.

At half past eight next morning, Tuesday, 21st January, I set off in grand style with Bishop Stuart and his wife for the journey to Gahini - the last lap of my journey to Ruanda! We went back along the road towards Mbarara till the fork for the frontier post at Kakitumba. The crossing was very swift and the Customs officials on both sides were most pleasant to us.

Ruanda at last! For some miles the countryside was very like the Game Reserve on the Uganda side, but then it became mountainous, with range upon range of rolling hills and deep valleys. The river Kagera, which forms part of the boundary between Ruanda and Urundi, flows right at the bottom of a very deep gorge. The road winds and winds down this for hundreds of feet, with many hairpin bends, then climbs up again. Lunch by the roadside was exciting! Then we had our first glimpse of Gahini, round a bend in the lake, Lake Muhazi. A wonderful welcome awaited us from Mrs. Allen, whose husband, a former medical missionary in the Congo, was holding the fort at the hospital while Dr. Joe Church was on home leave. Their daughter Peggy took me with her as she distributed milk and fish to the ulcer patients she cared for. We held a little service with them. They were people still suffering from the effects of malnutrition during the famine of 1945. They were friendly but so pathetic looking. After supper, Bishop Stuart read from *Daily Light* and Mrs. Allen 'broke bread' (as I wrote in my diary).

Wednesday was another full day spent in the car travelling to Urundi. We passed through Kigali (then just a small trading centre) and along the dusty road for many miles, till we stopped for a picnic under the black wattle trees just beyond the large RC Mission centre of Kabwayi. In the half distance a long bare-topped hill was pointed out to me, and I was told it was Shyogwe, where it was hoped to build up an 'Alliance of Protestant Missions' Education Centre. Little did I know then how often this place was to be my 'home'. Further south we came to Astrida, the Belgian administrative centre of the country (named after Queen Astrid of the Belgians) - now called Butare. We found the roads lined with crowds waving banners saying 'Soyez les Bienvenus!' ('Welcome!') However, they weren't meant for us, but for the Governor of Ruanda-Urundi and the Secretary of State for the Colonies who were due to visit Astrida that day. 'The shops there were full of a variety of things,' I wrote home, 'tinned fruits and fully-fashioned SILK stockings, wool and other materials - in fact, all kinds of things, though mostly very expensive. I visited the Administration Offices to see the District Commissioner in order to register as a resident or "Matriculate" as they call it. All the Belgian officials seem most charming and helpful, but when you try French on them they answer in perfect English!'

Some miles south of Astrida we crossed the bridge over the river Kanyaru that forms the boundary between this southern part of Ruanda and Urundi, and reached Buye at last. It was good to relax in a comfortable chair in the home of Dr. Kenneth and Mrs. Agnes Buxton and have tea. Good, too, not to have too many new faces at first! In the evening we met with the African conference delegates and heard reports of the work in their different areas. I slept that night in a tent in the Buxtons' garden and rejoiced in the quietness and solitude.

The following day, after a short service, I entered on my first duty as a missionary - preparing fruit salad and making sandwiches in large quantities! A meeting of the 'Alliance of Protestant Missions' in Ruanda-Urundi had been taking place, and when it was over we had an enormous spread and then sang till nearly 11 p.m. Present were a number of people from the two countries: Danish Baptists, Free Methodists from Canada, Americans of 'World Grace Testimony Mission', American 'Friends', and a Monsieur Faid'herbe of the Belgian Protestant Mission. (I remember being assigned to translate for him and discovering my French religious vocabulary was not as good as I had imagined!) All the different denominations seemed to have a time of real fellowship together.

After farewells to the 'Alliance' folk, we spent the next day getting ready for the arrival of the other CMS missionaries and African delegates, coming for the weekend Diocesan Council. I was assigned the task of typing out the minutes of the Alliance meetings, and also the agenda for the Diocesan Council (30 copies on a hand duplicator - those were the days before photocopiers or word-processors!) As the others began to arrive it was a great joy to meet up again with those I'd met in England, and to see those who had so far been only names to me. Joy Gerson arrived rather late, but it seemed only the day before that she had left me at Haywards Heath Station!

On the Saturday morning we had a fellowship meeting at which Dr. Algie (Stanley-Smith) gave us our 'Conference thought': 'We would see Jesus.' He shared with us the grave financial situation of the Mission and read the report of the Ruanda Council meeting. This stated that no-one could sail or be accepted for training unless their support was guaranteed. A certain amount of discussion followed this news, and much prayer. It was felt that the situation was a challenge to our faith rather than a discouragement: 'The Treasury of Heaven is never empty, and God only waits for us to be in a position of obedience.' At a later meeting it was agreed we must learn much more about prayer - the 'prayer that prevails.'

That night I had supper with Dr. and Mrs. Len (Sharp), Mrs. Guillebaud (Senior), Dora Skipper, Ruth Pye-Smith and Janet Metcalf. I felt I had arrived!

Chapter 3
Land of hills and valleys

Rwanda - the 'land of hills and valleys' - is one of the most beautiful countries in the world; a land of mountains and lakes, rather like Wales and about the same size; a land of rain-forests and game parks, with herds of zebra and antelope, lions and elephants; of wild savannah and volcanic mountain ranges, habitat of the rapidly decreasing mountain gorillas; a land of interesting flora, with giant lobelia, black wattle (mimosa), eucalyptus and many other varieties of trees - a fertile land with a normally good rainfall. When the Europeans first discovered the country they called it the 'Pearl of Africa', sometimes the 'Switzerland of Africa'. More recently it has been known as 'le pays des milles collines' ('the land of a thousand hills'). Meandering rivers, interspersed with lakes, flow through valleys fertile with the rich soil from hillside erosions. The highest source of the Nile is in Rwanda, where it emerges from the red soil of the high rain-forest. One of the country's most notable features has been its splendid long-horned cattle. It is also a country teeming with energetic people, being one of the most highly populated areas of Africa; in fact the population has more than doubled since I first went there.

Attempts to trace the origins of the inhabitants suggest that the great Bantu movements of the 7th and 8th centuries brought invading 'Hutu' with their agricultural economy to a land populated by a semi-pygmy race of hunter-gatherers and potters called 'Twa', who now became a minority in the reorganised country. National boundaries were not necessarily the same as the present ones, although they would largely have been dictated by natural features. In the 13th and 14th centuries other people moved down from the north in a further wave of migration; these were pastoralists called 'Tutsi.' They came seeking pasture for their cattle and spread throughout different areas of the country, imposing a semi-feudal system upon the Hutu, whereby the Tutsi received agricultural and other services from the Hutu in return for cattle and protection. Over the centuries these later immigrants (who greatly resemble the Nilotic peoples of the Ethiopian region in their height, bearing and physiognomy) assumed more and more authority in different regions, their leaders becoming known as 'Mutware' or Chief. Eventually, one leader over the whole country emerged and was known as 'Mwami' (King). Some of these became extremely powerful, at times extending their influence over parts of Uganda and other neighbouring countries.

For over 500 years it would appear that Hutu and Tutsi lived peaceably together, apart from the occasional injustice or abuse of power, in a mutually beneficial system, sharing a common language and culture. Intermarriage was not uncommon, and the concept of ethnicity was not generally divisive. However, as Rwandan society came into contact with changing sociological ideas of 20th century Europe, change was inevitable. It was, in fact, the 'scramble for Africa' and its resources that initiated the process of change which resulted in the polarisation of ethnic and economic differences that had previously been of little significance in the life of Rwandan people.

Upon unification under Bismarck, Germany felt she had missed out on the 'scramble'. At the Conference of Berlin in 1884, therefore, she was granted the 'Protectorate' of Tanganyika and Ruanda-Urundi, the area becoming known as German East Africa. Very little was known by either party about the other. Years later I heard, from one of the chiefs involved, how the then Mwami had called together his chiefs and warriors, telling them, 'I hear there are creatures approaching our borders with *pink* bodies! They must not be allowed to live, of course!' So he and his warriors went out with their mightiest bows and arrows against the Germans, who fired their guns and continued to advance till they had taken control of the country. The Mwami and his chiefs were allowed to carry on in their former roles; money was introduced to replace the old barter system, and the Germans built some roads and started some schools - their word for school being taken into the Rwandan language, 'ishuli'. During the First World War, Belgian troops from the Congo invaded Ruanda, driving out the Germans in 1916. After the War, the 1919 Treaty of Versailles re-allocated German possessions in Africa and Belgium was granted the Mandate, under the League of Nations, of Ruanda-Urundi, which they administered as one unit, though retaining their separate (Tutsi) kings.

The policy of the Belgians, as of the Germans before them, was to rule through the existing local leaders, a strategy which had the effect, on the one hand, of depriving them of some of their powers - for example, the Mwami lost the right of life and death over his subjects - and, on the other hand, of reinforcing patterns of chieftainship which had previously been exercised rather loosely. Prior to the European invasion, there had been division of power between those called 'Chiefs of the Soil' (Hutu leaders) and 'Chiefs of Cattle' (Tutsi), as well as 'Chief of Armed Warriors' (also

Tutsi). But by 1926 this pattern of power-sharing had been dismantled; Belgium now ruled through the most prominent of the chiefs, mostly (though not exclusively) Tutsi, whose authority thereby increased. Chiefs and sub-chiefs were used by the Belgian administrators as their agents in the work of modernising the country, with road-building, coffee plantations and other schemes. When work needed to be done, they would approach the chiefs, who then had to force the people (mainly Hutu) to carry out the work. This contributed greatly to the heightening of awareness of ethnic differences, fomenting resentment and growing antagonism, exacerbated by the Belgian policy of enforced registration, for which all inhabitants had to declare their ethnic grouping in their poll-tax books. Many Rwandans were of mixed parentage, and wrote down what they thought would be most advantageous to them at the time. If someone had a Tutsi grandmother and Hutu grandfather, for example, they would write 'Tutsi' on their forms, thinking that, as the Tutsi were being given ascendancy in the administration of the country, it would be most helpful to their own advancement and that of their children. Later, when the political situation altered after the revolution of 1959 which brought Hutu to power, some formerly registered 'Tutsi' remembered their Hutu forbears and had their poll-tax books altered accordingly - at a price! The Mwami (king) at the time of the Belgians' arrival, Yuhi Musinga, became increasingly unco-operative with Belgian policies, even subversive. He was also actively opposed to Christianity, threatening members of his family who showed an interest in being baptised. In 1931 he was deposed and replaced by his eldest son, Rudahigwa, through whom the Belgians believed they could rule harmoniously.

Meanwhile, Great Britain also had an interest in this part of Africa, a fact which had important consequences for the history of Anglican Christian missions in Rwanda

* * * * * * * * * * *

The influence of Christianity in Rwanda is comparatively recent; there is no evidence of any knowledge of it at all prior to the 20th century.

Under the German Protectorate, Roman Catholic missionaries from the order of the White Fathers (founded by Fr. Charles Lavigerie, the 'Apostle of North Africa') went to the Mwami for permission to start a Mission Centre near his palace. He did not deign to meet them personally (these *pink* people!) but he allowed them to settle further south, at Savé. Initially, they hoped to make Ruanda a Roman Catholic country, especially as Protestantism, and the Anglican Church in particular, was strong in Uganda, and at that time (before the Second Vatican Council) a certain rivalry existed. Their aim was to win over the King and the great chiefs, in line with their policy, 'Convert the leaders and the people will follow.' However, Mwami Musinga refused to have anything to do with the White Fathers, and not only refused himself to become a convert, but discouraged his chiefs from showing interest in the Catholics' teaching - an interest which they did, in fact, later show: the first Ruandan Roman Catholic priest was ordained in 1917 and in the decades that followed the Roman Catholic Church greatly increased its number of adherents. Rudahigwa, the king chosen by the Belgians, was already a catechumen; when he converted, the chiefs followed him. By the time I went out to Ruanda, all the chiefs except one (Ruhorahoza) and most of the sub-chiefs were Roman Catholics. Since the Belgians had come to power in 1919, there had been a great upsurge in the activities of the Roman Catholic Church; many schools and hospitals were founded, until eventually more than fifty per cent of the population were Roman Catholic adherents.

During the German Protectorate, Protestant missions had made a tentative beginning: two German pastors, Ernst Johanssen (1864-1934) and Gerhard Ruccius (1871-1940) were sent to Ruanda in 1907 by the Lutheran 'Bethel bei Bielefeld' Mission. Being German they had good relations with the government and the king, and over the next half-dozen years or so they established several mission centres. But after the Germans had been driven out, the German missionaries, now enemy aliens, had to leave. Responsibility for the mission centres was taken over by the Belgian Protestant Mission which, under Monsieur Henri Anet (who later proved very supportive of the CMS Ruanda Mission) developed educational and medical work at three centres - Kirinda, Rubengera and Remera.

About twenty years later, Danish Baptist missionaries extended the work they were doing in Urundi over the border into Ruanda, and later still some American Baptists began work on the borders. There was a Methodist presence too: Free Methodists from Canada began work in Urundi, then expanded round the borders of Lake Kivu to Kibogora in Ruanda. In the north of the country a group of Seventh Day Adventists had a well-established mission from 1922 onwards. These were, however, tiny minorities compared with the Roman Catholics, but together with the Anglicans these small Protestant groups in Ruanda later formed a Protestant Council - 'The Alliance of Protestant Missions' (now called the Protestant Council of Rwanda - Le Conseil Protestant au Rwanda).

The story of Anglican involvement in church growth in this Belgian-governed, Roman Catholic country of Ruanda is a fascinating one, and another illustration of the truth that 'God has ears'! The CMS had worked in Uganda since the 1880s founding churches and evangelising right up to the borders of Ruanda. They were a Bible-based foundation with a great spiritual burden for their neighbours and had a vision to move over the border into the country itself. In fact, historically the people of south-west Uganda had at one time come under the kings of Ruanda and spoke basically the same language, but boundaries made arbitrarily by the Europeans had cut them off from Ruanda.

The Anglican story proper begins with two doctors, Algernon Stanley-Smith (who was my first link with Ruanda) and his brother-in-law, Leonard Sharp. They had heard about Ruanda while still medical students; having read *In the Heart of Africa* by the explorer, the Duke of Mecklenburg, in which he describes the country and its people, they both felt that God was calling them to work there. But the First World War broke out, and after they had qualified they were called up into the Armed Forces. However, they offered to go as Medical Officers to Uganda and were sent to Mengo Hospital in Kampala. Through a misunderstanding on the part of the Ugandan Government they were granted permission to pay a brief visit to Ruanda (which was not officially allowed) while on local leave. Looking out over the hills and valleys of Ruanda they were even more convinced than ever that this was where God wanted them to come when the War was over.

In due course they were accepted as missionaries by the CMS, but owing to the severe demands on the Society's limited resources following the War they were asked if they would raise their own support. Consequently they gathered together a group of 'Friends of Ruanda' to pray and give financial support. They then set off in faith. Entry into Ruanda was forbidden at that time, as the francophone Belgian government was not willing to allow British missionaries from English-speaking Uganda to work there. Instead, the two doctors were located to Kigezi in south-west Uganda where, in 1921, they began medical work, at the same time praying with the Ugandan church, who shared the same vision, about the possibility of moving over the border into Ruanda. The possibility seemed remote, but they prayed, people in Uganda prayed, and the 'Friends of Ruanda' prayed. The result was an example of the miraculous ways in which God over-rules in human history.

At that time it so happened that Great Britain had plans to link Cairo with the Cape by means of a railway, which would run through the eastern part of Ruanda. Permission was sought, and granted, by international accord for Great Britain to take over that part of Ruanda. As soon as the area came officially under British rule, the two men sought and received permission from the British government to begin work there. (The man handling their application turned out to be an old college friend of Dr. Sharp's!) So in they went! Ugandan evangelists also took advantage of this 'open door' and began teaching and preparing people for baptism.

Half-way through 1923 Britain decided that the Cape to Cairo railway scheme was not practicable, so handed back that area of eastern Ruanda to Belgium. By now the British medical missionaries were well established; the Belgian authorities accepted the 'fait accompli' and made no objection to the continuing expansion of their work.

In that eastern part of Ruanda the first ever Anglican Mission Centre was established at Gahini, on the edge of Lake Muhazi, in 1925. The work was basically medical, but this was always seen as a spearhead for evangelism.

In 1926 the first baptism took place when eleven young men were baptised in the Anglican Church. From then on there was rapid growth; hundreds of people flocked to 'learn' (as instruction for baptism was called) and evangelists spread the work into the country around. Years later I asked one of the church leaders at Gahini, a canon, who was the son of a Ruandan chief and brought up in the old ways of ancestor worship and witchcraft, 'What did you think when you heard this message about God sending His Son to earth to show us His love and to die for our sins, and sending His Spirit to dwell with those who believe?' He replied quite simply, 'Something within me said, "This is the truth!" I remembered my own sense of that inner confirmation of the truth of the Gospel when I was in my teens, and marvelled at the wonder of the Holy Spirit's working in us in our very different circumstances.

How did those 'back-door' British Protestant missionaries continue to fare with the Belgian authorities? From time to time there was tension, and relationships would become strained, but an International Missionary Conference held in Belgium itself, to which Belgian Government Ministers were invited, helped pave the way (particularly through the contribution on behalf of the British missionaries, by Monsieur Anet of the Belgian Protestant Mission) towards improved relations between the CMS and the Belgian government. Two years later during the dreadful famine of 1928-29, one of the CMS doctors (Joe Church) undertook a great deal of relief work in organising food camps. Further, he had the perspicacity to write to the Ugandan newspapers about the famine - articles which were reprinted in *The Times,* thereby drawing international attention and subsequent international famine relief to Ruanda. Improved relations culminated, in 1930, in the granting of official status - 'Personnalité Civile' - to the CMS Anglican mission: an important day for Anglican work in Ruanda!

A year later came another even more important day - the arrival of the New Testament in the vernacular, Kinyarwanda, translated by Harold Guillebaud (Peter's father), who later succeeded Arthur Pitt-Pitts as Archdeacon of Ruanda-Urundi. Two new centres were opened, one in the north at Shyira, and one in the west at Kigeme. The country was opening up through contact with Europeans; goods were being imported: watches, bicycles, shoes.... People were eager to learn to read; ability to read was a prerequisite for baptism into the Church as it was important that Christians should be able to read the Scriptures for themselves. People flocked into the churches. It soon became apparent that if they hoped for work in the country they needed to be baptised, because schools and hospitals were run by the churches, there being comparatively little government work in education or health care at that time.

People also flocked for healing. Dr. Stanley-Smith was known by the Africans as 'Imana y'ibimuga' ('the God of the cripples'). He carried out amazing operations on people with twisted limbs and other deformities. When people attended hospital, the doctors and other staff would talk to them about the Christian faith: people would walk miles to reach the Christian hospitals, often passing by the government ones, because, they said, you got more than just physical help, and you did not have to bribe the staff to look after you well, as was often the case at government hospitals. They appreciated being prayed for before having an operation. And they were genuinely eager to hear the Gospel, and often responded warmly. At Shyira in the north, patients would walk or be carried many miles up the valley and climb the thousand feet to reach the hospital. One day, I was taking the prayers at the Out-Patients Clinic and started to tell the story of the Prodigal Son. The folk were sitting in rows on the brick benches, poor people mostly, some still wearing bark-cloth or skins as they could not afford to buy cloth. (Bark was split off from the wild fig trees, and beaten until softened, then used as cloth.) When I got to the point of the story where the Father looking out sees his son coming back and rushes out to embrace him, they all clapped, exclaiming, 'Yakoze cyane!' - 'How well he did! - and 'N'igitangaza!' - 'How wonderful!' I realised it was the first time they had heard that story (this was in the late 1940s). It seemed wonderful to them that the father would forgive such a son and receive him back with such joy. It was simple to tell them that God does just that with *his* children as they repent and turn back to Him.

Rwandans were very receptive to the Gospel message, not just for the benefits it brought them, but because of their own concept of God and His relationship with the world. Like many Africans before coming into contact with western secular thinking, Rwandans believed in a Supreme Being they call 'Imana' who created the world and everything in it, and was closely involved in human affairs. But something went wrong and He went far off. They have various myths about how this came about, and the stories all show some kind of disobedience on the part of His created beings. They recognised, as Christians do, various attributes of God, e.g. Almighty, All-seeing, and use descriptive idioms such as 'Imana Igira Amaboko' (literally, 'God has arms', i.e. He is powerful) and 'Imana Igira Amatwi' (meaning 'God has ears', i.e. the God who hears). Though He has distanced Himself, He is still the ultimate resource: when all else has failed, they say 'Hasigaye Imana' - there is still God left. They did not conceive of God as merely a local deity; he was universal, but he was the God of Rwanda, as their saying goes: 'God may spend the day elsewhere, but He comes home to Rwanda at night.'

So to hear that God loved humankind, and sent His Son to bridge that gap between them and Himself, was good news indeed!

However, because they believed that God had gone far off did not mean they were not conscious of other forces around. The spirit world was very real to them, as to many Africans and non-Christian peoples who have sometimes been called Animists, or more exactly, adherents of Primal Religion. The spirits of the ancestors were believed to have an influence in many ways, so they had to be placated by offerings of food and drink placed in special little shelters, otherwise they might do you down. Some of the earliest national ancestors (reported in legend) were thought to live on the top of the volcano Muhavura, and most Africans would not climb far up that mountain in the early days of the Christian Church. The power of witchcraft was much feared. Spells and curses put on people seemed to have very real power to harm. So, when they heard that Jesus, on the Cross, had overcome all the powers of darkness, and defeated them, it was wonderful and relevant news! They were able to prove in personal experience that the power of Jesus was greater than that of spells and curses, was greater indeed than all the power of the evil one. People tested the reality of their new faith, and saw it work. The Gospel really was Good News!

'An African Nebuchadnezzar'

Chapter 4
Revival

Revival was still spreading rapidly when I arrived in Ruanda. The CMS Ruanda Mission were celebrating their Silver Jubilee, and were looking forward eagerly to the expansion of their work over the next twenty-five years and beyond in all departments of their work - church, medical and educational.

My first years were spent in training teachers, at the main Mission centres of Kigeme, Shyira and Shyogwe. Initially I spent a month at Shyogwe with Joy Gerson and Hilda Langston, helping on a Refresher Course for men teachers previously trained by Peter and Elisabeth Guillebaud. 'I'm not much use, of course,' I wrote to my parents; 'I don't know enough of the language to make a simple sentence yet, though apparently I manage to pronounce words reasonably recognisably. Some of the sounds are very difficult to reproduce though, and the grammatical rules seem endless, but everyone is most helpful and they say things very slowly!'

Letters I wrote in this early period give a good flavour of what life was like, and of my experiences and impressions. I describe some visits, including one to the kraal of the widow of the great chief, Semugeshi (the former chief of the Kigeme area whose story is told in *An African Nebuchadnezzar*): 'The chief's younger children, who are in Joy's care, are all with us and are so nice. We go out for walks each evening and they show me things all the way along; then they come and read with me to help me get the sounds.

'Last Sunday we took them to visit the Queen Mother, to whom they are related, and had a most interesting time at her Palace. It is rather a curious brick building with four towers like oast houses at the corners of the enclosing wall, inside which is a fairly ordinary kind of large bungalow with wide verandahs. The rooms had the most luxurious skins on the floor, leopard, monkey, etc, that your feet just sank into, and the walls were decorated with coloured designs in blue and red. The furniture was quite European and there was a very English-looking tablecloth in drawn thread work. Of course there were several examples of native craftsmanship, especially lovely baskets and bowls of woven grasses so fine as to look like silk and with such interesting patterns on, and others of the finest bead work, again very wonderfully patterned. They also showed us a very old spear that had belonged to the King's grandfather - it was very long and, again, both it and the sheath were beautifully decorated. She, and indeed so many of the people here, looks so very like the Ethiopians and so many of their customs and traditions are the same, that it seems almost certain that their own stories of their migrations from the north hundreds of years ago must be true.

'Today we went to visit the local chief here at Shyogwe. He is quite young and is one of the many whom the Belgians have substituted for older men who have not had such a European background. He is most friendly and helpful and took us over his new house, which he is just having built - a brick one and such a change from his present one, though that was beautifully built in native style.'

A letter dated two weeks later, the 1st March, 1947: 'Our time at Shyogwe at the Refresher Course is nearly at an end, and we shall be returning to Kigeme next week. It has been really grand here, for the men are so terribly keen to learn all they can, and some of them are exceptionally good with children. They have given practice lessons to children from the day school here and I have had great fun trying to criticise and give suggestions. Then we've taught them some of our team games for each age group, with singing games for the young ones especially adapted to fit in with things they know, e.g. "Oranges and Lemons" is all about cows - still the most important thing in the country. "Farmer's in his Den" is about someone who is ill with toothache, earache, or a broken leg, etc, and is taken to the hospital. Then instead of "we all pat the dog", they make the doctor come along and cure them all - much more sense than our version, I think.

'One day last week we all went on a visit to the big RC Mission station a few miles away and had a very interesting time there. First we were taken over their printing works and saw printing, bookbinding, etc, including quite a number of lino cuts of English scenes that were sent over as British propaganda during the War. The men students were thrilled with it all, as most of them hadn't seen anything quite like it before. Next we were taken over the museum and spent a long time there. An African Padre (later an Abbé) called Alexis Kagame took us round and told us much of the history of the country, which is recounted in a long and very beautiful poem, rather like Homer or the Old Norse Sagas. Very few people know it, and it is passed down from father to son among a special

Oranges and lemons

family that can speak a form of the language that is not easy for foreigners, or even many Ruandans, to understand. Father Kagame has managed to write down much of it and translated it into excellent French verse. He is a brilliant man - one of the cleverest in the country - and has helped in the writing of the history of the country. This has just been published and they let me have a copy. It is in Kinyarwanda so in reading it I kill two birds with one stone - learn some past history and learn some Kinyarwanda. The story of the kings goes back to the 14th century, but before that they have discovered traces of quite an advanced society, with metal weapons and some bricks with queer markings that may well be writing. It is amazing how foolishly superior Europeans have been in imagining they have the monopoly of skill and brains - they would soon get a rude awakening if they heard some of Kagame's own poetry (French and Kinyarwanda) or saw some of the amazing patterns that are done in the finest bead and basketwork.

'Another day we had a visit from three very high-born chiefs, who came and talked of their early memories of the country before the Europeans came, then of the coming of the Germans and what they thought of them. One of them had been forced into the German Army during the War and had been one of forty whom they taught to use a gun. They are such gracious, courteous people, tall and very handsome, that it's no wonder they didn't think much of Europeans when they first saw them!

'Another day our local chief brought a man along to play an "inanga" to us. This is a stringed instrument which they play to accompany their stories and songs, of which they have very many - in fact they make up songs about everything, and the tunes are delightful, but almost impossible to reproduce - at least I've not been able to do it yet!

'We paid another visit to the Queen Mother the other day, as some of the students wished to say goodbye to her before they leave for other parts of the country. She is really the 'hand behind the throne' and it is impossible to get anything from the King, or even see him, without first seeing her. Apparently she is rather a tartar in her way and may keep people waiting at the Court for weeks without seeing them. After we'd chatted a little she took Joy off for a private chat and left me with four great ladies, all beautifully dressed in brightly coloured cottons and with their hair dressed very high. They tried to teach me many words and get me to pronounce them properly, but some sounds I can't get at all. They of course speak the purest and best Kinyarwanda in the land. After a little while the Queen Mother called me in to show me the crowns which are worn on special occasions. They are made of the most beautiful beadwork, with fur round the top. She agreed to put hers on and let me photograph her. Then I took another of the King's by itself on a table. I am very fortunate to have seen so much already that very few Europeans have seen.'

After that month at Shyogwe came a year at Kigeme, beginning serious study of the language and helping to run a Teacher Training Course for girls with Joy Gerson. We had sixty boarders from all over Ruanda-Urundi. The girls had already received some primary education, which they continued with us, and we trained them to teach children of kindergarten age and primary years 1 and 2. I had language study for several hours a day, including conversation sessions with a young man who had been educated in Uganda, so spoke good English. Very few people yet spoke French (the official language together with Flemish), so one was forced to learn the vernacular, Kinyarwanda, which of course is the best way to really get to know people. We were required to pass two language exams before we could come 'off probation' and be voting members of the Missionary Committee in the country.

It was such an enjoyable time of getting to know the country and its people. The climate was pleasant, even cool at times, and we spent occasional free days by Lake Kivu, about 50 miles away through the high rainforest, swimming in its clear, safe water - no crocodiles, no bilharzia. Kigeme itself was at a height of 7,000 ft. above sea level on the edge of the rainforest. 'It certainly deserves the name of "Switzerland of Africa",' I wrote home, 'for the hills are very high and close together with fast-falling streams in the valleys. There are quite a lot of trees, mainly black-wattle (mimosa) and eucalyptus, with banana plantations here and there.'

The following year (1948) Joy and I moved north to Shyira, to help run a new mixed Teacher Training Course for thirty men and thirteen girls, training them specifically to teach children in primary years 1 and 2. We obtained official government recognition as an 'École d'Apprentissage Pédagogique' for our two-year course. To have official EAP status was an important stage in our educational work, and also for the students' status later as teachers eligible for government grants.

Then next year it was back to Shyogwe, where I joined Peter and Elisabeth Guillebaud at the new École de Moniteurs (four-year Teacher Training College) and a new Sixth Form College - Sixième Préparatoire - for specially selected students, most in their upper teens from all over Ruanda-Urundi, being coached for entrance to the only secondary school at that time in the country, the École de la Charité at Astrida (Butare) - a Roman Catholic school run by the Frères de la Charité - which required a high standard in French. This had recently been declared by the government open to students other than Catholics. (At this time school entry depended on the student's level of education rather than chronological age, so many entered school as mature students.)

These were years of rapid church growth, and the education network developed rapidly in tandem. Schools sprang up in the village churches and there was constantly an increasing demand for more of these. In view of this it was important that teachers were given a sound general education alongside good pedagogical training, since our Mission Schools were now eligible for government recognition and, therefore, 'grants in aid' for qualified teachers and equipment, provided they reached the required standards. As a result, we also became subject to government inspection. I had come to Ruanda at the initial stages of this educational development. People previously received little or no formal education as we understand it; reading and writing had only been introduced with German colonisation and had not become at all widespread. In 1921 an Anglican evangelist had come down from Uganda and started teaching the Gospel, also reading and writing. Some of his pupils had been sent along by the local chief who was so embarrassed when the government officials sent him messages in writing and he could not read them, that he wanted these young men to help him in this. By the time I left Rwanda at the end of the '60s, tremendous progress had been made: Rwanda had several secondary schools, run by various church denominations, and its own university at Butare, having adapted readily to Western-style education.

These were years, too, when Revival played a central role in our lives. Regular meetings for prayer and fellowship, as well as large conventions, became woven into the pattern of life. I loved the warm and stimulating fellowship of my African colleagues in church and school, and felt enriched by all that I learnt from them. At different stages of my spiritual journey I would tend to feel satisfied that I understood all there was to understand about a particular aspect of my faith, until one of the African Christians would bring some truth alive in a new way.

I had found in Ruanda, as in Urundi and East Africa generally, a church full of joy and praise and singing. At first I adopted a slightly patronising attitute towards this, thinking to myself, 'Yes, I remember being like that when I was first saved, but I'm more mature now of course!' Such spontaneity I associated with the childhood days of new spiritual birth and I'd noticed that people in England seemed to grow out of it. But as time went on, my encounters with African and other Christians in the Revival fellowship led me to abandon my former attitude, and gave me new insights into the reality of the faith by which I thought I was living. I have never forgotten an early conversation I had with Yosiya Kinuka, one of the pioneers of the Revival and one of only three ordained African clergy in the whole of Ruanda-Urundi at that time. He was from a cattle-owning family in Ankole, Uganda, and having suffered badly as a child from severe ulcers, had been given the name Kinuka, which means 'bad smell'! He had sought treatment at Kabale hospital and subsequently became a hospital worker there, and later at Gahini. During our conversation he asked me, 'Mademoiselle, do you know the power of the Blood of Jesus?' Somewhat indignantly I replied, 'Yes, of course I do!' Hadn't I spent years in Crusaders singing, 'There is power, power, wonder-working power in the precious Blood of the Lamb'? But he went on, 'Do you really, in daily experience, know that power to give victory over sin, wrong thoughts, depression? Also, are you proving continually that once you have brought something to that cleansing Blood it is gone, and you must not let the devil or anyone else bring it up again?'

This practical awareness of the power of Jesus to break the power that things had once held over their lives made me understand why people praised and sang so much about the cleansing power of Jesus' Blood - it was an everyday miraculous reality for them.

Some days previously, Eustace Kajuga, one of the Shyogwe schoolmasters (later ordained) had come into the Guillebauds' house where I was staying and said, 'I've just had to repent of jealousy, and been forgiven, Glory to the Lamb!' Often I heard people repenting of such things as jealousy, or resentment, and thought, 'Poor things! Are they still only at that stage? I'm never jealous!' I considered it an immature, even despicable, reaction. But then Eustace had told the details of the circumstances that had given rise to his jealousy, and I realised I had had the same reactions to the situation he was describing only I had not recognised it as jealousy or as a sin of which I needed to repent and from which I needed to be cleansed and freed. God then began to open my spiritual eyes to other reactions that needed to be called 'jealousy'. I became aware that I was actually jealous of another missionary recruit, older than me and of a different educational background. I considered myself something of a linguist and was setting about learning the language methodically, paying attention to its intricate grammar. This colleague would just blurt out greetings and other phrases people had taught her, and I could hear her making awful grammatical errors and not getting the tone right; whereas I hesitated to say anything at all until I felt confident I was saying it correctly. So I was rather annoyed when one of the African schoolteachers said to me one day, 'Why don't you try and speak more, like So-and-so does? Is it pride?' 'But she gets all the agreements wrong', I thought to myself. Then I realised it *was* pride that was at the root of my reticence to speak until I could do it without making mistakes, and that I *was* jealous of my sister in Christ and the way she was praised for her efforts. After my conversation with Pastor Yosiya, I prayed for forgiveness and claimed the power of the Blood of Jesus to cleanse me and break the hold of the sin on my spirit. It is hard to put into words what happened, but I just knew that my previous reaction to her had gone, and the power of the jealousy was broken. I could understand why my Revival friends sang with such joy, because I really did feel set free from an attitude that could have spoilt my relationships with others, and I was filled with a sense of deep joy. Of course, this was not a 'once for all' experience, but the beginning of a path of continual repentance, and cleansing. Through the many testimonies that were given in the fellowship meetings and in church, I found I was becoming more open to the Holy Spirit's convicting work, showing me the inner sinful attitudes that were as serious as actual wrong words and deeds, and needed to be repented of as such.

People were very sensitive about any hint of sexual impurity, and would frequently repent quickly of wrongful thoughts or fantasies, following Our Lord's warning that the thought is as serious as the deed (in Matthew 5:28). The wonder of continual repentance, continual forgiveness and joy, was highlighted for me by someone's testimony of having had to repent of the same thing repeatedly, and praying, 'Oh Lord, I've done it again,' and of hearing the Lord say, 'Done what?' - which brought home to him the truth of the Scripture: *'I, even I, am he that blotteth out thy transgressions for mine own sake, and will not remember thy sins.'* (Isaiah 43:25).

Critics of the East Africa Revival sometimes referred to us as the 'Sin and Say So' group - a slick phrase that implied we did not regard sin as being serious; but the reality was quite different.

The Revival brethren were very good at giving apt illustrations of spiritual truths. William Nagenda said to us one day, when the question of continual repentance had arisen, 'You know the windscreen wipers you Bazungu [Europeans] have on your cars,' - this was years before many Africans possessed cars themselves - 'which continually wipe away the water when it's raining? Well, that's a picture of the Blood of Jesus, continually cleansing us so we can see clearly the way ahead.'

Julia Barham, wife of Lawrence Barham (one of the early leaders in Revival and later Bishop of Ruanda-Urundi), told me of a conversation she had had with Pastor Yosiya Kinuka during which she had asked him, 'What colour is your heart, Yosiya?' He hesitated a moment before replying, 'White, through the Blood of Jesus,' and then went on to explain, 'I paused for a moment to bring to Jesus anything that might have sullied me so that I could be cleansed.'

In one of the early great conventions which became such a feature of the Revival fellowship, Dr. Joe Church was led to give a message based on Isaiah 35:8: *'And a highway shall be there, and a way, and it shall be called The Way of Holiness; the unclean shall not pass over it ....'* We could walk that Highway together, he said, as we continually asked forgiveness of God and one another. Set free from those sins which can vitiate the life of a community if left to fester, we felt very safe with one another.

The 'way of holiness' was a way of 'light', and this imagery became very important in our corporate and individual lives. Being open about oneself and having nothing hidden or wrong between oneself and others in the fellowship, became known as 'walking in the light': *'If we walk in the light, as he is in the light, we have fellowship one with another, and the blood of Jesus Christ his Son cleanseth us from all sin.'* (1 John 1:7). This walking in the light often involved repenting in public, especially if the wrongdoing had affected others or had been publicly known. In church circles in England there was criticism of the whole revival movement because to those hearing reports second-hand, it seemed inappropriate for certain things to be shared openly. But in those times of fellowship there was a compelling power of the Holy Spirit to put things right with God and others, that one kept quiet at the expense of one's spiritual well-being and peace of mind, knowing one had 'grieved the Holy Spirit'. In those days I was very reserved in temperament, yet under the compulsive power of the Spirit I would frequently find myself on my feet, confessing sins and omissions, some from years before that the Spirit brought to my mind, and seeking reconciliation with people with whom I had been unkind or even untruthful.

Walking in the light also involved telling one another, in Christian love, if we saw anything in their words or actions that were not the 'highest' (another much-used metaphor) or that would hinder Jesus being seen in them. On one memorable occasion, at Shyogwe, a mature African student-teacher taught me a lesson I never forgot. We were running a Teacher Training programme which included practical classes in agriculture, for which we used hoes, which cost a good deal of money out of our limited resources. I was in charge of these agriculture demonstrations (a fulfilment of my early ambition to be a farmer!) and tried to keep the equipment in good order and stacked neatly when not in use. But at the end of one particular session, the students rushed up to the shed flinging in their hoes in a jangled mess. I knew that when they tried to pull them out next time they would get damaged and the heads come off. 'Stop!' I shouted. 'Come back here! Stand in a line! Now, go into the shed one by one and carefully pull out a hoe, then put them back properly so that they're not jangled up.' There was a shocked silence, and looking rather abashed they did as I'd said. I returned to my house feeling rather pleased with myself. A little more discipline was what was needed around here!

At the end of the week, there came a knock on my door. Timothy, a small fairly young student, though already married, was standing there. 'Mademoiselle,' he began, 'I have come to ask your forgiveness.' 'Oh?' I said, 'What about?' I could think of nothing he had done to offend me. He went on, 'I have not been really helpful to you at all this week. I have let you down.' 'Oh?' I said again rather foolishly, at a loss to think what he could possibly be referring to.

'You see, I have waited a whole week and have not had the courage to come and say this to you. When you told us about putting away those hoes last week after our agriculture lesson, you lost your temper. Some of these students are not saved, they don't know Jesus, and they do not see Him in you when you lose your temper.'

'But I didn't lose my temper,' I explained. 'I was just laying down appropriate standards for the proper care of school equipment. We have so little financial resources and I am responsible for the right use of these.'

'But that is what it looked like to us,' he said. And I thought to myself, 'If that is what it looked like to them, that is what I have to respond to, and put it right.' So at the beginning of the next lesson with that group, I said, 'I want to ask your forgiveness for speaking to you as I did about the hoes. It was not the way someone who belongs to Christ should speak to people.' There was never any trouble over the hoes after that. And in fact an entirely new, more unified relationship was created between us.

It was true Christian caring and faithfulness, and the willingness to accept it, that gave one a sense of freedom and safety, because whatever you said or did would be quickly challenged if it was not 'highest', and fellowship maintained. So there was no lengthy building up of anger or resentment or harbouring of grudges. Dr. Stanley-Smith once said to me, 'I have come to realise that it is not what I thought I said, or even what I know I said, that I must react to, but what other people thought I said.' It has been a helpful insight for the whole of life. If people don't think you said what you thought you said, it is what they thought that you have to deal with!

Silas, a schoolmaster at Shyogwe where I was based as Schools Supervisor for the area, came along to my office one afternoon. The custom on all the Mission/Church centres was to meet for about half an hour morning and evening, usually in round specially-built prayer houses or huts (called kazu), for prayer, reading a passage of Scripture, sharing insights, repenting and putting right anything that might have gone wrong. But at this particular time I was very much occupied with government reports (as we were now receiving grants for schools that reached the required standards), so I had not been along to the prayer times for a while as I was feeling so much under pressure.

On this particular afternoon, Silas came in and said, 'I've just come to say that for the last couple of weeks you've been nothing but a government servant.'

'Well, I *am* a government servant, virtually! The Mission gets a subsidy for me, and I have all these reports to finish.'

'That was all I wanted to say,' he replied. 'Thank you. Good-bye!'

Burdened with the pressure of paperwork, my immediate human reaction was one of self-pity and seething resentment at his accusation. But in my spirit I knew there was a difference, which he had detected, between just doing my job and living in the Spirit within the joy of fellowship. So I picked up my Bible and went off to join the others at the prayer house, trusting the reports would all get finished in time!

This 'putting someone or something in the light' was a prominent feature of the Revival fellowship at that time, and could be a very good test of one's humility and openness! But, like all spiritual movements, it could get out of balance. Sometimes dissatisfied or truculent younger schoolmasters, for example, would criticise or challenge seniors inappropriately under the guise of 'being in the light'. Then again, some church workers or missionaries did not feel easy with living in this way, and so the fellowship began to exercise more discernment. William Nagenda told me one day that he had learnt through the years to be clearly guided by the Holy Spirit about what he 'put in the light' and with whom.

As time went on, the leaders in the big conventions were very careful about whom they allowed to stand and give testimonies in public. In the early days anyone could leap to their feet and speak, but as meetings became much larger, sometimes people abused this freedom and things were said that were not led by the Spirit and could be unhelpful or divisive. But, led by the Spirit, it was a wonderful way of deepening fellowship and mutual understanding of the amazing grace of God.

Another insight that undergirded the safety of fellowship was to do with stamping out gossip. At one of the early conventions I attended at Gahini, Bill Butler, then a missionary in Uganda, challenged us not to go to sleep at night if there was anything that needed to be put right with God or man. Particularly he stressed the importance of always telling another, either face to face or by letter, if we had spoken about them to another person, especially if it was a negative comment; for example, 'I was talking to So-and-So, and said that I thought you were rather aggressive, or handled a particular situation badly. I'm sorry, please forgive me.' Then, if the remark was passed on to that person - 'So-and-So said such-and-such about you' - they would be able to say, 'Yes, I know. He/she told me, and we are at peace about it.' I found that 'keeping short accounts' with people really did help us to walk in harmony and freedom in our fellowship and work. Again, if we did hear critical remarks being passed on about another, we would say to them, 'Have you told that person face to face? Because if you haven't, I will.' This proved a very effective way of stemming gossip and negative critical attitudes within such a close community.

'Brokenness' was another term that became part of the Revival vocabulary and way of life in the whole movement that was increasingly becoming known worldwide as the Ruanda Revival - or, more accurately, East Africa Revival, as far more of the international leaders, in fact, came from Uganda than from Ruanda-Urundi. Dr. Joe Church composed this chorus which we used to sing:

> *Lord, bend this proud and stiff-necked I;*
> *Help me to bow the head and die,*
> *Beholding Him on Calvary*
> *Who bowed His head for me.*

It was another way of expressing true humility; a willingness to say 'I'm sorry,' without making the excuses, 'I was tired' or 'I was provoked,' but just admitting, 'I was wrong, forgive me.'

One day, while at Shyogwe, when we had some large building projects going on, I was standing nearby when Peter Guillebaud walked past and noticed that some work had not been done properly by the African builders. He turned back and tore metaphorical strips off them for their slack workmanship, as he saw it. But after walking on a few steps, he turned back and said to them, 'I'm so sorry, I should not have spoken to you like that. Please forgive me!' and continued on his way. I overheard one of the builders turn to the others and comment, 'The Christian religion must be real if it causes a European to ask forgiveness of an African!'

Sadly many Europeans adopted an attitude of superiority over Africans. Even some missionaries did not think those they had come to teach had any right to question them. When the question was put, as it had been to me in my early days in Africa, 'Are you saved?' the reply of some white Christians would often be, 'My dear young man, I have been a Christian for x number of years,' or 'I was saved in 19--.' These remarks were usually followed up by the response, 'It's wonderful what happened to you all that time ago, of course, but is Jesus saving you now?' The Africans' deep concern was for one's present walk with God - a walk which ought to preclude the 'high horse' approach!

One particular Ugandan schoolmaster, later ordained and a great leader in the Revival, was travelling with me in a milk van one day when I was on my way for a few days' visit to Namutamba, a large tea plantation and cattle ranch which had become a centre of the Revival fellowship and the venue of some of the great 'Balokole' conventions. In the midst of my sharing with him details of my spiritual journey, he interrupted me, saying, 'Oh yes, we'd heard you weren't broken.' He was making the distinction between being born again and being broken. I was discomposed by his remark.

A few weeks later I met him again and said to him this time, 'I must repent of having felt upset by your remark about my not being broken.' Not letting me off the hook easily, he replied, 'Yes, I thought you would be!' This type of challenge was what we called the 'hard light'. But on looking back I was grateful for his faithfulness, for I realised I was something of a rebel, reluctant to 'toe the party line' and tending to question things that others just accepted. This was possibly at the root of his remark that people felt I wasn't broken, and the challenge helped me towards a deeper humility for I realised that if I were asked 'Are you broken?' my reaction should not be, 'How dare he ask me that!' but rather, 'What must my life look like, or indeed be like, if they need to ask me that question?' I was learning more about the Way of the Cross, and it was very humbling.

One day this same schoolmaster came into the lounge at the Kabale Preparatory School to join us for tea. Kabale was such a lovely place for a holiday, so various people from other parts of Uganda were staying. One of the Preparatory School teachers had a friend in secular employment who had come down from Kampala for a holiday; this headmaster, having been introduced to the visitor, sat down next to her and asked, 'Are you saved?' Her friend - as were some of the rest of us - was horrified. But the visitor replied, 'No, but I'd so much like to be. Can you help me?' And he gently showed her the way! Where there is sensitivity to the leading of the Spirit, as he clearly had on that occasion, obedience to that prompting is greatly blessed. But it takes courage!

I suppose this 'brokenness' is really the attitude described by Paul in Romans 12:3, where he says a Christian should not think of him/herself more highly than he or she ought to think. Yet it must not be a false humility. I remember being challenged one day by Sara Nagenda, William's wife, when I said I was no good at something or other. 'Don't despise yourself!' she admonished me, helping me to see there was a balance between recognising that I was a person with gifts and of value to God, and thinking myself better than others while verbally protesting my insignificance. It was easy in Africa to acquire an inflated sense of one's own importance when first of all you have a white skin, and secondly you are in a position of authority, and you feel you have seniority and experience and do not like people with less talking down to you. But it comes down to the same sin of pride, and lack of humility.

That is not to say, of course, that other people are necessarily right in what they say: they may indeed be wrong; but it is one's own reaction that matters. Their words or actions are their responsibility before God, though there is a place for gracious challenge when all are walking 'in the light'. There is even a place for 'hard light' with those with whom one is in really close fellowship, and at that 'safe place' of trust and love in Christ.

Pastor Yona Kanamuzeyi (whose story is told in the book *Forgive Them*) said to me one day, 'I saw you through my window this morning as you were walking along to teach at the college, and thought you looked defeated, not walking in the joy of the Lord.' It was true, and made me think, 'Yes, it matters very much how one walks and greets people, in spite of how one may be feeling.'

Another time, when I was 'Directrice' of Schools in the Kigeme area, one of the teachers from an 'out-school' looked in on me to greet me. I was absolutely inundated with work and blurted out that I was busy. He pointed out, quite rightly, that a smile only takes a second - no longer than a frown and a gruff response. I remembered a comment I had heard about Dr. Stanley-Smith: 'When you call at his office,' they said, 'however busy he is he moves the papers on his desk to one side as he smiles and greets you. You feel you matter to him. Also, you try not to disturb him for too long!'

It was a young kindergarten teacher, a girl of about 16, who gave me another very helpful insight into 'openness' and 'walking in the light'. She commented one day, 'We must not dare put something in the light with someone until we have been to the Cross with it ourselves.' This has often returned to challenge me, and I've found that by doing this, very often the situation clarifies itself in my mind as I pray and I feel I don't need to say anything after all, but if I do still feel the need to speak to the other person, I find the manner of my approach is different from what it might have been and such that they are able to accept the challenge more easily.

Indeed, I owe so much to the insights and helpful challenges of the African women. One area of behaviour that I have never forgotten was that of our appearance as being part of the 'highest' - only the 'highest' being good enough for God, a concept that can have a transforming effect on standards of work and other things, including our appearance! This went counter to much of the Christian teaching of my background and the attitude of some of my senior missionary colleagues. An early illustration of this came from a girl student in our first Teacher Training course. She questioned me one day about the wardrobe of one of the other missionaries who always wore very plain garments, almost like a uniform. She had brought back from England several green nurses' type dresses which she wore in school every day. 'Has Miss So-and-So only got one dress?' I was asked. 'No,' I answered, 'she has several all the same.' 'Whatever for?' she exclaimed, horrified at the idea. I went on to explain that she did it so as not to make the African girls envious because they had so few clothes. 'How ridiculous!' she burst out, 'What does she think it's like for us to have to see her standing up in front of us in that dull old thing every day? We love to see pretty and different things. It cheers us up and gives us ideas of how to dress.'

Another point of contention was my hairstyle! When I was home in England I had become used to having my hair permed, but had been advised by senior women colleagues that I should not try to do this in Africa as the change in its appearance between perms would trouble the Africans and it would 'stumble' them to hear that I had things done to it artificially. Indeed in the early years of Revival there had been a phase when any elaborate hairstyles, both for men and women, had been rejected by the African Christians themselves. But while on one of my 'furloughs' (our times of home leave) I met Sara, when she and William were on a speaking tour in England. 'Doreen,' she exclaimed, 'how nice you look! Why don't you have your hair done like that in Africa?' I told her the reason. 'Stuff and nonsense!' she said, 'It stumbles us much more when you appear not to bother with your appearance when you're with us, when we see photos of how you look at home. We feel you think anything is good enough for us, and that is very hurtful.'

So I learned another important lesson, that while it is of the utmost importance to understand and comply with cultural patterns and sensitivities, it is essential to realise that these do change and modify through contact with others and other influences; one must not harden into patterns that are no longer appropriate for a new situation. Indeed, it has often been the pattern of the Christian Church down the centuries to harden into a mould which, though appropriate when first developed, can become a hindrance to the ongoing work of the Spirit. A good example of this was seen in parts of Uganda in the '60s. The injunction to 'make a joyful noise unto the Lord' in the Psalms led to the blowing of trumpets and other loud instruments in church meetings and in the areas around. At first, when it was spontaneous and joyful, it contributed to the sense of worship and was uplifting. But it developed into a cult, whereby trumpets always had to be blown, and those who did not do so were considered 'unsaved'. What had been an inspiration became a divisive ritual with no life in it.

Some of the criticisms that arose about the Revival teachings arose because of this very same hardening into patterns, not only by the fellowships in Africa, but by those who followed what they thought was the way to revival blessing in England and in other parts of the world where people from East Africa went and shared testimonies of what was happening. There was too often a slavish copying of patterns of worship and behaviour that had 'worked' in Ruanda and elsewhere under the direct leading of the Spirit of God. But practices adopted as mechanical 'rule of thumb' techniques do not necessarily produce spiritual results in a different time or situation. 'Walking in the light' and 'the way of brokenness', if carried out as a ritual, could cause misunderstanding and hurts; whereas, led by the Spirit of God, they brought peace and unity among us.

Chapter 5
New insights in Belgium

In order to qualify for a government subsidy and be recognised as head of an educational establishment in Ruanda-Urundi, we were required to spend a whole year in Belgium, studying the Belgian education system, following an intensive French course led by a professor of Brussels University, and completing the Colonial Course required of all Belgian officials in the Congo and Ruanda-Urundi. This latter included a wide range of useful subjects, from the history of Belgian colonial administration in Africa, to Anthropology and Tropical Hygiene. Previously the government had given grants only to Belgian directed schools (which meant mainly Roman Catholic ones, though there were three Belgian Protestant Mission educational establishments which also received help); in 1946 however, the new Socialist government in Belgium changed this policy and extended their recognition and grant aid to any school attaining the required educational standard and whose head teacher had completed the Brussels course and qualified as 'Professeur.'

From a spiritual point of view, my year's compulsory residence in Belgium (from 1952 to 1953) proved to be a very significant time, for God led me into a deeper understanding of the Biblical teaching on the Holy Spirit. 'Keswick' teaching had laid sound foundations in my early Christian life: if one is born again, one is born of the Spirit and can claim fullness of the Spirit, which I had done. In East Africa the Revival teaching was very Jesus-centred: the focus was on the saving work of Christ on the Cross and his cleansing Blood; but rarely was there any direct teaching on the work of the Holy Spirit. On one occasion, I remember Dr. Joe Church had said to us, 'If you are cleansed in the Blood of Christ, there is no barrier to the filling of the Holy Spirit in your life.' He returned to this teaching in one of the large conventions where the theme was 'Cups Running Over' - with joy in the power of the Spirit. A vivid picture was given of God moving among us to fill us, but sadly passing by dirty 'cups'. To be continually filled with his Spirit we needed to be continually cleansed by the Precious Blood. These were wonderful Bible truths. However, from time to time I was puzzled by certain New Testament passages about the 'gifts of the Spirit' and 'Baptism in the Holy Spirit'; but when I shared these questions with others in the Revival fellowship I would be told, 'We have it all in Jesus - what more do you need?' Nevertheless, the questions stayed at the back of my mind, and I felt there was teaching in the New Testament that I was not appropriating for myself.

While in Belgium I stayed with a Belgian Pentecostal family, who regularly provided accommodation in their Brussels home for 'foreign' students going as missionaries to Belgian dependencies in Africa. Pastor Neusy, his wife and two boys made me feel one of the family - in fact it was a very lively household, with three of us from the Colonial Course billeted there: the two others were Swedish Pentecostal girls, going to Urundi. The family did not speak any English, which was a great help in our quickly becoming fluent in everyday French, and Madame Neusy was particularly careful to help and correct our grammar and pronunciation. Living there, and hearing news of their church and its outreach, gave me an insight into the 'pentecostal' scene in the early '50s, before the charismatic movement became widespread in the States and Britain during the '60s.

Every weekend we were visited by another Pentecostal pastor working in Brussels, Carlo Johanssen, who was Swedish. Both men impressed me, an outsider, as being deeply grounded in the Scriptures, and belonging to what appeared to be the only group really cutting any spiritual ice in Belgium (which was predominantly Roman Catholic) at that time: other churches just did not seem to be reaching out in a way that was making any impact on non-churchgoers, whereas these two pastors were holding open-air meetings in the market place and making contact with people from various walks of life.

One day Pastor Johanssen asked if I would like to come with him to share in ministry at his church, in another part of the city. When I expressed some doubts on the grounds of being an Anglican, he wrapped up years of church history with a dismissive, 'Oh, les petites différences!' For him I was 'persona grata' as a born-again Christian, even though I wasn't familiar with the Pentecostal phraseology or ethos; so I went with him and shared my testimony, feeling a sense of oneness in the Body of Christ. Coming back in the tram, we had to sit some way apart, but as he caught my eye at one point he mouthed the word 'Halleluyah!' - and I felt reassured and accepted as a sister in the Lord!

Several times I went along to church with the Neusys, though usually I worshipped with the Belgian Protestant Church along with most of my fellow Colonial Course students, most of whom were American. At

Pastor Neusy's church I heard for the first time people 'speaking in tongues', either individually with an interpretation, or corporately in what was a truly worshipful experience. There were also testimonies of physical healing, which did not have a place in most evangelical churches at that time. Certainly we prayed for people when they were ill, that the doctors would be given wisdom in their treatment, and in the Ruanda-Urundi hospitals patients were prayed for when having operations, but there was little mention of the 'gift of healing' of which Paul wrote: and there was an underlying feeling that concentration on physical healing might side-track people's focus on 'Jesus only'. Protestants of my generation had become very cerebral in our beliefs; we accepted, indeed, that they rested on faith and not on feeling or proof - but did we really believe in the supernatural, or expect it, in practice, to impinge on our everyday world? The accepted teaching was that divine intervention in physical matters - miracles and supernatural phenomena - ceased in the apostolic age. However, when praying for financial needs, and receiving answers to our prayers, many of us did have testimonies to share. It was my contact with the Pentecostal churches in Brussels that gave me my first-hand evidence that God does still intervene in miraculous ways in the physical realm.

My mother died suddenly while I was in Belgium - a victim of the terrible smog of 1953 in London, which clogged her lungs and caused 'cardiac decompensation.' I had only just received my sister's letter saying Mother had been taken to hospital but that the doctor had said there was no need for next of kin to be called, when a telegram arrived saying she had died. It was a great shock as she had always been so full of life and energy, and was only 63. I returned home for the funeral in Reigate Parish Church, spending a few days meeting up with family and friends. Some of my Christian friends queried the rightness of leaving my father on his own and returning to Ruanda. But when I suggested to him that I should stay at home, he said, 'Don't take this the wrong way, but I'd prefer you to go. I've always thought it quite wrong for the older generation to hinder the calling of the younger ones.' As a seal on this, my sister Ruby said she felt it would be right for her and her family (her husband Patrick and children Andrew and Jennifer) to move into my father's house, as she felt called to keeping house anyway, and it would make me feel at peace about leaving him, which it certainly did.

Back in Brussels I received kind and sensitive support from the Neusys and Pastor Johanssen and his wife. While visiting them one day he asked me 'Do you have the gift of tongues?' In amazement that he should think that I, a rather strait-laced evangelical, might be pentecostal, I shook my head. 'I thank God every day for this gift,' he said to me; 'it is a great blessing to my soul.' I was puzzled. 'Whatever does he mean?' I thought; but his words impressed me deeply. He was a man I had come to respect for his spiritual insight and powerful ministry, and I could not forget his remark.

About this time Pastor Johanssen invited me to join in a mission he was holding in Sweden and other areas. Again I was surprised, and when he said he felt that the message of the East Africa Revival would be a helpful contribution to the mission, I was eager to go. However, we were very much subject to authority in those days, so I mentioned the possibility to my senior missionaries. Not being so relaxed about 'les petites différences' they told me I must not consider such a venture. The East Africa Revival did not feel it right to be associated with Pentecostalism, which my joining in the mission might seem to imply. I was somewhat astonished that I was considered important enough to be noticed in this way, and disappointed at what I was beginning to see as a negative attitude to other Christian groups who were going forward in evangelism. Surely those experiencing different expressions of God's blessing should rejoice and work together? My study of Church history, however, had shown me that often a fresh move of the Spirit of God finds its greatest opposition from the one immediately preceding it. Leaders often fail to recognise that as situations change there is need for a different aspect of the whole counsel of God to be highlighted to meet current needs. But, even though I realised this, I felt constrained by the fact that a younger - and female - member of the Revival fellowship did not presume to launch out on her own unless she had checked with the leaders first - always men!

Our Course in Belgium involved quite a bit of travelling around. We visited many schools, observing their teaching methods, including agricultural colleges to study their farming methods. We also studied the judicial system, even visiting courts of law, and climbing to the top of the Palais de Justice.

Public health, too, was focussed on, and we were taken on a tour of the (wonderfully constructed) Brussels sewers!

I came to love Belgium and its people, and found on my return to Ruanda that the experience helped to form a bridge in my closer working with the Belgian officials, who loved to hear someone who appreciated their own homeland. Fluency in French had also improved, for though I had studied it at University and had started to teach it in our schools in Ruanda, it had not been really colloquial. There was, of course, a strong linguistic divide between French and Flemish in Belgium, and this was extended to the African dependencies: all official documents were in both languages; so I came to recognise written Flemish fairly well.

At the end of the year I received my accreditation as 'Professeur' and prepared to sail back to Africa, to face whatever awaited me there.

Chapter 6
Revolution and Refugees

I took back with me to Ruanda many memories and some deep questions. I was hesitant, however, about sharing my interest in the 'gifts of the Spirit' and the whole Belgian experience at all widely, as I heard that a team of leading brethren (African and English) had recently been on a mission to the Congo and had been troubled when they encountered Africans who claimed to have 'charismatic' gifts, yet who did not seem to have experienced new birth in Christ. On their return to us they openly shared their reservations about 'pentecostalism'. I remembered, too, the concern there had been a couple of years earlier when a new missionary came out to Shyogwe and had given her testimony about receiving the 'gift of tongues.' (She shared my house with me in Shyogwe, and had also lived with the Neusy family in Brussels.) I was interpreting for her when she gave her testimony, and the brethren had asked me, 'But has she experienced the power of the Precious Blood?' At the time I felt rather sorry for her, thinking she had got off on the wrong foot as it were, and the brethren would be uneasy about her, yet I did notice that she seemed to have a freedom in the Spirit and an authority when she preached that others soon came to recognise too. Later I felt free to share with her some of my own experience, but for the time being I put the whole subject of 'gifts' aside and prepared for a new assignment - at Kigeme again.

The educational network was increasing rapidly as the desire for education grew and grew. I was appointed 'Directrice' in charge of the primary schools at Kigeme itself and also of those that were springing up in the large district around. Each area covered by a Mission Centre was divided into districts, each district having its own senior evangelist responsible for a dozen or more small village churches with its own local evangelist or catechist, who taught people (young and old together) to read in preparation for baptism. It was in these rural churches that the demand for primary schools was growing. Visiting and assessing, and trying to equip these schools, entailed much travelling on foot, up and down the steep hillsides and wading or being carried across fast-flowing rivers, camping with my little 6 ft. by 6 ft. tent in church compounds, and sharing rich fellowship with the local Christians and church leaders. Now that we were able to apply for government grants, it was essential that we establish full-time primary classes following the recognised syllabus, and that the large number of new teachers required should receive some formal training. At Kigeme I started a training class for senior girls - a venture of faith as there was no official recognition or grant available. But Bishop Jim Brazier, who was based at Kigeme at the time, encouraged me in the venture and gave us a gift from a personal fund he held, and other friends at home contributed as we prayed, though our needs were modest. The girls slept in one of the old schoolrooms of the one-time Kigeme Girls' School, cooked their own food, and made their own teaching aids. Later on I was able to obtain official recognition, retrospectively, for the course, so the teachers could be eligible for a subsidy providing the class they taught qualified for one. To qualify, at least fifty per cent of the pupils in a class must obtain at least fifty per cent of the marks in exams and continual assessment in the year. This meant that even if a class qualified for a grant, we received no money until well into the following year after all the reports of all the classes (which it was my responsibility to collate and submit to the government) had been examined. We were always, therefore, having to find funds in advance for salaries and equipment, so we learnt to improvise in various ways.

On Saturday mornings I would call in the teachers from the out-schools, as well as those on the Mission Centre, to prepare materials for their classes the following week. For example, to help familiarise children with weights and measures, we would find long sticks, cut them into metre lengths, then mark off decimetres and centimetres on them; look for stones or bricks that weighed a kilo, etc; mark a litre level on a jar, or half a litre on an empty tin can. I used to beg empty tins from my fellow missionaries as they could be put to so many uses, such as making little drums (from Cerebos salt tins) painted and tied round with string, or filling empty talcum powder tins with small stones to make rattles for the kindergarten children's percussion band! For art lessons we used earths of different colours, and for brushes we would peel off the hair-like fibres found inside the stem of banana plants. Newspapers (again begged from colleagues) when whitewashed could be used for drawing paper, though sometimes we used the walls of the classroom (if there were any!) for drawing and painting topical themes as they could be whitewashed off again later. Initially many classes did not have buildings, but gathered under large trees or a simple shelter. The church building would be used for the senior class, with the children sitting on brick benches or on the floor. Gradually more classrooms were constructed, often of mud and wattle, with thatched roofs. For blackboards the wall would be plastered and smeared with a mixture of cow's blood and soot from the cooking pot! Because of the shortage of writing materials we often started the small children with pointed sticks in the sand to give them a 'feel' for writing. They then progressed to slates and slate pencils, before graduating to pencils and exercise books, which were in very short supply. In fact, for some years I had to order such equipment from Belgium and got quite proficient at handling bills of lading and going down to Bujumbura, the Burundi capital, to collect the crates that had travelled all the way up the Congo river after shipment in Antwerp. Later we used to buy from the large RC Mission centres, when they began to run wholesale stores for all kinds of goods.

At the same time as rapid expansion of school work, evangelism and church planting continued at a fast pace. Especially in the dry season when not much could be done in the fields, teams of Christians would go out on the hills and share the Gospel in open-air meetings or at church centres. Sometimes there would be weekend conventions at larger church centres. We would camp or be put up with local Christians who provided hospitality. For these services, and always on Sundays throughout the year on the Mission Centres, we would meet for half an hour before the service to pray and prepare for ministry. We would share any 'word' we felt God had given us for the day, i.e. something from the Bible or a testimony of some convicting word of God. Then we would pray and share what we felt God was leading us to include in the time of ministry, and who should expound the Bible passage, who lead, who give a testimony, etc. After the teaching part of the service, time was given for others to share a word of encouragement, give a testimony or start a hymn of praise.

It was truly a team effort, with no rigid division between leaders and congregation, though the senior church workers, teachers and hospital workers took overall responsibility for services. In fact evangelism and educational work and medical work was all one, some of the hospital workers being outstanding preachers. One such was Eriya Kabarira, head of the Kigeme hospital staff, himself originally a missionary from Ankole. He was particularly gifted at finding vivid relevant illustrations in his sermons, and used my flannelgraph board pictures to great effect. Rarely were there any ordained clergy available - in fact there were still very few in the whole of Ruanda-Urundi so they had to travel round large areas taking Communion services, very rarely at the same place within weeks. But the church grew in spite of (or, I might almost say, because of) this, and the fact that church members really saw it as their responsibility to share the Gospel with their neighbours and to build up one another in the faith.

One year I went on a three-week joint medical and church-planting 'safari' to the south-western area of the country. Josephine Stancliffe, then Nursing Superintendent at Kigeme Hospital, and some of the African staff nurses held clinics at the various places where we camped, while I joined a senior church leader, Andereya Sempiga, to measure up sites for new churches. We would cycle or walk along hillside tracks to the place where a group of local residents had asked for a church and meet with the people and the local chief. The owner of the land would state before his neighbours and the chief that he was donating the plot for the church. I would then pace out and mark the area, normally half a hectare (about 50 yards by 50 yards), and draw a map of the site, showing the surrounding landmarks. When we had marked out all the sites in that district (ten on that particular safari), I took the maps to the Belgian Administrator for official recognition and copying in triplicate. He checked that there were no other claims on the land, or other obstacles to a church being set up there. The papers, duly signed by him, the local chief and me, were filed in his office; one copy came to us and the other was filed centrally. Years later I visited some of those same sites that I'd originally measured and found they were flourishing district centres, with their own clergy, and some of them still having my original maps!

With Josephine Stancliffe

Each day when we returned from these church planting visits, I would rejoin Josephine at our camp site and we would gather together with the local Christians in worship and witness at what God had done, then share a meal together before finally retiring to our tent. We had taken along our cook who helped us in the house at Kigeme, to make us breakfast (over an open campfire) and help with general tidying, etc. One day, on my travels with Andereya, I spotted some edible field mushrooms, and whooped with joy as I thought of the tasty addition they would make to our breakfast. As I was picking the mushrooms here and there, Andereya drew close and said, 'If you must eat those disgusting things, at least need you publish the fact abroad so blatantly!' I learned a cultural lesson - the Tutsi, being cattle people, did not eat mushrooms, though the pygmies did, because they said they grow where the cows have urinated!

These were wonderful and inspiring times (apart from the mushrooms!), with so many people coming to a living faith in Christ and witnessing to their neighbours, and with the consciousness of our deep oneness in the Lord.

After nearly four years at Kigeme I was moved to Shyira, where Dr. Godfrey Talbot-Hindley and his wife Phyllis had built up a very lively fellowship. Godfrey had taken over as Field Secretary from Dr. Stanley-Smith, who 'retired' to Uganda to help with the translation of the Ankole Bible. In the hospital Godfrey was assisted by a senior nurse, Marjorie Wheeler, who did much to build up the high standard of nursing of the African staff in our Mission hospitals. I had the privilege of sharing her house for a while and beginning an enriching friendship which lasted throughout our years in Africa and later back in England. Here at Shyira, as at Kigeme, I was Directrice of the 'Centrale', i.e. the schools on the Mission Centre, as well as supervising district schools and opening up new ones, which again entailed much 'safari' work - and here the hills were even steeper! I continued helping teachers with their visual aids and teaching materials on a Saturday morning, and sometimes we did field work in connection with the teaching of Geography. One memorable weekend we went north to the area of the great volcanic mountain range that we could see from Shyira, and climbed the easternmost peak called Muhabura. This can be seen from most parts of Rwanda, a fact which earned it its name, literally meaning 'it makes you unlost' - in other words, the 'Pathfinder'. It is over 13,000 ft. high, and on its slopes the great mountain gorilla have their home, though sadly many have now disappeared through poaching and encroachment on their forest habitat.

We started out early in the morning from one of the out-schools where we had spent the night with the catechist's family. The school itself was about 6,000 ft. up, which only left us 7,000 ft. to climb! We walked up the steep paths, through shrub-land, plains of giant lobelia, bamboo forest, then out on to steep grassland. The world we looked down upon looked strangely remote and unreal. Just below the last steep climb to the summit, my legs began to drag heavily and I could not keep up with the young schoolmasters, who then *ran* on to the top, soon returning with a bottle of water for me, taken from the lake in the crater at the summit!

My first car – Volvo 'Sports'

Towards the end of 1958 I had a short leave of five months, during which I visited supporting churches and built up much closer links with my home church, St. Mary's, Reigate, in Surrey. They adopted me as their official 'Own Missionary', as Mission Partners were then called. Some time later they held a garden party to raise money for my first car, which made such a difference to my schools supervisory work, especially when I became Education Secretary for all the Anglican Mission Schools in both Rwanda and Burundi. It was while on this furlough that I noticed a change in the attitude to women speakers in many of the churches I visited. Whereas previously I had been invited into church halls to speak, or occasionally I spoke from the chancel steps in the church, this time I found that in many of the churches, particularly in the north of England, I was obviously expected to preach from the pulpit, and this became the norm on future visits.

Even more interest was added to this furlough by 'Expo 58', an outstanding experience. At this International Trade Exhibition, held in Brussels, the Protestant Alliance of the Congo and Ruanda-Urundi were allocated a corner stand in the 'Congo' Pavilion. I was privileged to spend three weeks helping to staff this stand, along with a schoolmaster from Urundi, Samweri Sindamuka, whom I had taught at Shyogwe Teacher Training College. He liked to take up his position near the display of Bibles printed in the different languages of the Congo, Ruanda and Urundi, and as people passed by he would say, 'Would you like to hear a reading from my own language, Kirundi?' Then he would read a verse, usually John 3:16, *'For God so loved the world, that he gave his only begotten Son, that whosoever believeth in him should not perish, but have everlasting life,'* and translate it for them. One day I was standing near when a group of Belgian men gathered round him. 'What are you, an African, doing following the white man's religion?' they asked him; 'You have your own religion and culture.'

Sam smiled down at them from his height of 6 ft. 6 inches, and said, 'Sirs, may I first ask you what you know at first hand about our religion and culture? I am an African, and proud of it, but I also know that there was much in our traditional customs and practices that was not helpful, and that we were dominated by fear of evil spirits and witchcraft. Then I heard of Jesus Christ and his victory on the Cross over all the powers of darkness, and came to him in faith and found peace and joy. And, after all, it isn't the "white man's" religion, is it? Jesus Christ himself wasn't white, was he? He died for the sins of the whole world. May I ask if you have accepted him as your Saviour?' At that, they turned away thoughtful.

This was how Sam, and so many of those Africans who were truly born again, shared their faith graciously but clearly wherever they went. Later, Sam trained for ordination, quite soon became a bishop and eventually Archbishop of Burundi, maintaining a courageous and inspiring witness, especially during the times of ethnic tension and violence throughout the '90s.

But, in the late '50s, such thoughts of violence, or even genocide, were far from our minds. By July 1959 I was back at Shyira, sharing a house this time with Josephine Stancliffe, who was now Sister in charge of the hospital while the Hindleys were on leave. However, in November Revolution burst upon us.

Outside Shyira Hospital [right]; Josephine Stancliffe [left]

The King, Mwami Rudahigwa (Mutara III), had died on 24th July 1959, in mysterious circumstances. According to the official medical report he had died of a brain haemorrhage, but it was widely believed that he had been poisoned. He had been on the throne 28 years and was very well respected. He was succeeded by his nephew, Ndahindurwa (Kigeri V), chosen by the 'Abiru' (those who 'know the secrets' - in this case, of the succession) in accordance with Rwandan tradition; a young man who was welcomed with terrific enthusiasm as he travelled round the country making himself known to his subjects. When he came to Shyira I remember people were so excited; in fact our Mission Centre was not on his official itinerary, but he insisted on coming up to the top of the hill where we gathered in front of the hospital. It was one of those spontaneous highly-charged moments as we all burst into applause. I shall never forget the sensation - I felt it was almost as we would feel at the Second Coming!

But the change of monarch at this point in the nation's history only contributed towards the break-up of stability due to the changes taking place within society. The former King had held the country together in a widespread feeling of loyalty, though he himself had introduced reforms that led to the break-up of the old feudal network called 'ubuhake' (literally meaning 'doing obeisance to'), which had survived for over 500 years. Cattle, which had been the basis of the feudal relationship, were divided up according to a system whereby the overlord retained one-third and the agricultural worker retained two-thirds, in return for the service he had given the overlord through the years. The Hutu, therefore, were no longer obliged to cultivate land or do other work for the (mainly) Tutsi overlord, which had the effect of changing the way in which they related to each other. The traditional pattern of interdependent loyalties and social links and ties was disrupted within a very short space of time; by 1955 it had virtually disintegrated.

Expansion of education contributed significantly to this and other changes. By the late '50s many more secondary schools had sprung up in line with Belgian policies of development. In the earlier years the few post-primary establishments founded by the various denominational missions had of necessity been boarding schools where fees needed to be charged, so they tended to include mostly the children of richer Tutsi with very few children from Hutu families who could afford the fees or do without their children's help in the fields. Now with more schools, children could often attend by day, so more Hutu and poorer Tutsi children were able to attend. In the schools they learned more about their history, and were introduced to the idea of democracy and equal rights. New ideas, new economy, new opportunities - all jostled together in a heady combination which spelt 'amajyambere' - progress! And in an era when colonial empires were breaking up there was much talk of independence, particularly when Belgium proposed independence for the Congo. Educated Hutu realised that if independence were to be granted to Ruanda while current political structures were in place, with mainly Tutsi exercising authority as chiefs of different areas, then they themselves would have little opportunity of acquiring political power or status. Consequently some of them formed a political party - the Parmehutu (Parti d'Emanicipation des Hutu) - to challenge Tutsi dominance while the Belgians were still in control.

Support for the Parmehutu spread like wildfire - as did the flames of Tutsi kraals burnt in reprisal for the alleged murder of some Parmehutu leaders. Tutsi cattle were taken or slaughtered, and though people themselves were not generally being killed at this stage, unless they resisted, many homeless Tutsi fled to various centres such as churches, schools and hospitals.

One morning as I came back to my house from visiting the primary school at the other end of Shyira Mission hill, I met folk running up from the market below. 'Mademoiselle!' they called out, 'Terrible things are happening. People are burning Tutsi houses, killing their cattle, and threatening to do the same to us if we don't join in!' Just as they were saying all this, a shout went up. 'Look! Another kraal being attacked!' I'd reached the verandah of my house by this time, and looking down the valley below I saw smoke beginning to rise from the house of Frederic Shabukuru, one of the Tutsi schoolmasters, while a group of men tore out the doors and windows of his brick-built house and ran off with them. Brick or mud walls made little difference to the attackers, except that thatched roofs responded more readily to the match. Soon all around as we stood watching, columns of smoke began to rise up on the hills round about us. Suddenly we were in the middle of what proved to be a revolution! Within an hour hundreds of people had fled to what they felt was the safety of our Mission Centre, carrying pathetically small bundles of what possessions they had managed to snatch up. We lodged them wherever we could. I opened up the school classrooms for them to doss down in for the night, others found shelter on the hospital verandahs or in the homes of the mission staff.

Later on that evening I received a message from our local sub-chief, Michael Kibugu, a committed Christian who had had an amazing conversion some years before - he had fallen to the ground under the power of the Holy Spirit and had a vision of the Lord on the Cross. He and his wife had been threatened with mutilation or death, and he had heard that the 'rebels' (as they were considered at that time) were coming that night to burn his kraal. The message said, 'Can we come and take shelter in your house, because they are not attacking white people.'

Here was a dilemma! By giving shelter to the sub-chief would I be putting at risk not only my own home, which I shared with Josephine, but also the homes and possibly the lives of others at the Mission Centre? I was on my own at the time because Josephine had gone in her car, with Erasto Kinyogote, a senior evangelist, to drive the 120 miles through the night to Gahini to tell them of the dangerous situation we were in and seek advice and help. (We had no telephone or radio, and no way of knowing if the same things were happening elsewhere.) I finally decided that, without Josephine's assent, I could not risk what might well be the destruction of our home and property if we gave shelter to the sub-chief, so I told the messenger that, regretfully, I could not receive them. Just before going to bed, however, as I was praying, I felt the Lord bring to me very clearly his words in John's Gospel: *'Greater love hath no man than this, that a man lay down his life for his friends.'* (John 15:13.) I felt that I had not been willing to risk my own security for my friends' sake, and that the thought of Josephine's property was not my basic reason for refusing sanctuary. So immediately I called a messenger nearby (a Hutu friend of the chief) to say that I would, after all, welcome his wife and children, but that I felt he himself should try to get away from the area under cover of darkness. Within half an hour came a tap on the door: they had *all* come! So I directed them to an inside room with no windows, which we used as a bathroom. It contained a tin bath and jugs but no running water. I filled the jugs with water, gave them food and a primus stove, and chairs and cushions to sit on; but I omitted to warn them not to open the door unless they heard my voice. Early next morning my house-girl knocked on the door. They opened it, and were discovered!

That day being Sunday, we held a short service on the hillside near the primary school buildings, and were very conscious of God's overshadowing of us. We knew that all around us armed bands were gathering, and heard them blowing their horns (made from cows' horns) to gather people together. The burning of kraals continued, including some of those of Mission workers beyond the perimeter of the Mission compound.

Early in the afternoon came a message from one of the groups of raiders. As missionary in charge of the Mission Centre they wanted to see me! Accompanied by Edreda, the wife of the evangelist who had gone with Josephine, I went down the road to meet them waiting for me at the hairpin bend on the edge of the Mission property. I was greeted by a band of men with spears and staves. They wanted my permission to come on to Mission land so that they could seize various Tutsi who were in hiding in Mission buildings. (It says something of the respect in which Mission Centres were held at that time that they would bother to ask for permission!)

'Why are you hiding our enemies?' they demanded to know.

'I don't know anything about "enemies",' I replied; 'I have come to share with everyone the Good News of Jesus and his love for all people, and I'm not involved in any political issues.'

'We know that's what *you've* come for, Mademoiselle,' they said, 'but Yona Sekimonyo, the headmaster, has disappeared and we believe the Tutsi have killed him.'

As I stood there, an Englishwoman of 5ft. 2in. surrounded by these armed men, I experienced a strange kind of detachment, as if it was a play I was looking down upon.

'Of course they haven't killed him!' I replied (though I had no idea where he was or what had happened to him). 'And I cannot allow you to come on to this hill if you are intent on killing. This is God's hill!'

'There is no God, Mademoiselle!' said one young lad, thrusting his face near mine.

'Oh yes, there is! And you will see that He will not allow you to come further up this hill, if your intentions are to kill.'

I was amazed to hear my own voice saying these words. 'Lord,' I prayed silently, 'there's only Edreda and me standing here, they have only to walk past us.' But they didn't! They looked at one another and then turned to leave, threatening, 'If the headmaster isn't found by tomorrow morning we will come and get the culprits.'

As we returned up the hill we passed the hospital and found that one of the schoolmasters, Eustace Rutiba (later to become a Professor at Makerere University in Uganda), had gathered the refugee children together on the verandah and was leading them in singing choruses! I felt I must warn the refugees at the hospital of the impending danger, and encourage them to try to escape when it was dark. We prayed together, committing ourselves into God's hands. We knew that the armed bands of attackers were lurking around, but we believed also that other, invisible, bands (as seen by Elisha's servant in 2 Kings 6:8-17) were surrounding us too - for there was no human reason why those raiders should not have attacked a Mission Centre protected only by one woman missionary!

I returned to my own house as dusk was falling, and was met by Michael, the sub-chief, and his wife Bereta. 'It's not right for us to stay and put you in danger,' they said, 'so we are leaving, and will try to get out of the country.' (They eventually managed to escape to Uganda, where they spent some time before finally settling in Kenya.)

Then a note was pushed under my back door. It was from the headmaster. 'I've heard of the difficulty you are in. I did go into hiding as I heard my life was in danger - but I'm not going to continue to put you in jeopardy because of me, so I'm coming back.' Full of thankfulness for his courage and concern for us all, I sent off a message to the raiders (there were several people acting as go-betweens), saying that the headmaster was safe and well.

Soon afterwards Josephine returned from Gahini with Ted Sisley, one of the other missionaries, and our pastor, Andereya Sabune, who had been away on holiday. They told us that the Belgian authorities had promised us protection and were posting soldiers on our hill. These arrived the next morning and turned out to be half a platoon of Congolese troops. We praised the Lord who had saved us from a terrifying situation when we faced the possible loss of property and numbers of lives. As earlier I had faced the prospect of losing all my possessions, and even my life, I realised that nothing must ever matter to me again except to preach the Lord Jesus and to bow to his will in all things. The *Daily Light* reading for that night (8th November) was so wonderfully appropriate: '... *the children of Israel pitched before them like two little flocks of kids; but the Syrians filled the country.... I will deliver this great multitude into thine hand, and ye shall know that I am the Lord.*' (1 Kings 20:27-28.) And '... *they shall not prevail against thee; for I am with thee, saith the Lord, to deliver thee.*' (Jeremiah 1:19.)

The raiding bands were still around in the area, and as they came near the Mission hill again the soldiers fired, killing one of the raiders. This had the unfortunate effect of increasing the hostility of local Hutus to the Tutsi refugees, whom they blamed for the man's death. I myself had not been too happy when the soldiers arrived as I felt the protection of the Lord was far safer than that of armed soldiers, and this result of their coming reinforced my feelings. In the circumstances we felt it unwise that the refugees should stay any longer on our property, so Dr. Harold Adeney, a senior medical missionary who had arrived from Buye, having heard of our situation on the mission radio, went down to the government post at Ruhengeri about 20 miles away to ask the Administrator if transport could be provided to take the refugees to Uganda. We had heard that the Governor of Uganda (still under British rule) was willing to accept unarmed Ruanda refugees. The Administrator agreed to this request, and the following morning at 6 o'clock seven lorries arrived to transport them, accompanied by one of the Belgian officials. It was a sad sight to watch as, dazed and despairing, people climbed on to the lorries clutching their bundles of belongings: many had been quite wealthy with well-furnished houses, land and cattle, but they left their homeland with virtually nothing.

Harold Adeney and I went with the convoy, in his car, so that we could make arrangements for their reception across the border. But when we reached the frontier post, the Uganda officials on the other side refused to admit the refugees, saying, 'You can't bring these people across the border, they have no passports.' We explained that we had heard that the Governor of Uganda had said that unarmed refugees would be allowed in, and they replied, 'Yes, people fleeing for their lives with spears at their backs, but not whole lorry-loads of people being driven across!' However, after some further discussion and explanations, they agreed to send a radio telegram to the Governor in Entebbe, to ask his advice. Meanwhile Harold and I, being possessors of British passports, were able to cross the border and fetch food for the stranded refugees. We experienced again God's wonderful over-ruling providence when, making a short detour, we met Bishop Kosiya Shalita, a Rwandan who had been brought up in Uganda and who had years previously been one of the pioneers of the Gospel in Ruanda-Urundi. He was now Bishop of Ankole-Kigezi (the border area), and was able to facilitate all the preparations for housing and feeding the refugees once they'd crossed the border.

Back with the refugees again we waited for hours, and as we waited the Belgian customs officials said, 'I'm afraid these people will get badly drenched, as we always have a heavy storm about 2 o'clock these days.' There was no shelter and the refugees had spread themselves out over the open ground. Soon clouds did begin to gather, and drenching seemed inevitable as the storm approached. Then, as we prayed, we saw the clouds parting in the middle, and the storm passed by on each side of us. We had only a few drops of rain, while on either side of us it poured down in torrents.

At last we saw a motor bike approaching, ridden by a British police officer. He made a 'thumbs up' sign, for he had brought the reply from the Governor: 'Yes, we could go in!' But a further problem now arose. The Belgian administrator accompanying the lorries said he had no authority to allow the lorries to travel into Uganda - it was five miles to Kisoro, the small town where the refugees could find shelter - but only to take them to the frontier post. However, more prayer and tactful pleading, until he finally said, 'Well, if I get a rocket so be it. Okay, let's go ahead!' Arriving at Seseme, the Anglican church centre close to Kisoro, we found the Christians there, who had been told of our arrival by the Bishop, were all ready to welcome the refugees. They had opened up the church schoolrooms and spread dried grass over the floor for bedding, and obtained food from the local hotels. Most of the Tutsi refugees were Roman Catholics, and were very moved by the kindness of the Anglican Christians. Once they were settled, Harold left for home, but I stayed on with them for a while, as they did not speak English and it was necessary to have an interpreter.

This time spent on the border regions of the two countries had its enjoyable moments, for I was able to join in an expedition to see the mountain gorilla on the slopes of Mount Muhabura, joining some other Uganda CMS missionaries who were on holiday in the region. We started out early after breakfast with African trackers, and climbed to where the gorilla had had their breakfast. Then we followed their tracks up and down the mountain slopes and into the bamboo forest. It was raining slightly and was very slippery, and after some of this clambering along, I felt that even if I never saw a gorilla, at least I now knew what it felt like to be one! We stopped for lunch, and soon afterwards the guide suddenly said, 'Stop! Look there!' and through the bamboos we saw a group of gorillas. As they saw us, they barked like big dogs, and I felt my heart beating rapidly. Though in my mind I wasn't afraid, I decided I didn't want to go any nearer! However, the guide pushed us on, saying, 'Haven't you come especially to see them?' Soon the gorillas turned aside and made off into the forest. We had another glimpse of them later as we skirted an open clearing, a family of them playing together.

Ten days later I went back to Shyira, and was astonished to discover that Josephine and I were front-page news in England! A *Daily Express* reporter in Uganda had intercepted the radio telegraph message sent to the Governor in Entebbe, and had rushed up to Shyira for details. The result was an article in the *Daily Express* with the headline, 'Women Defy Killers!' The article was a sensational (and inaccurate) report of how we had confronted the rebels. My photograph had the caption, 'She bandaged wounded', and was accompanied by a description of how I had torn up my sheets for bandages, which I certainly hadn't - there were no wounded to bandage! In the next day's paper I was astonished to read an account of my early life, details of which bore no resemblance to my own memories of it, and to see another photograph with the caption, 'She Shunned Dances'. A letter from my sister Ruby explained everything: the newspaper had rung my father for information about me, which he had refused to give, and then had contacted her for background information. Apologetically, she confessed that it had taken her by surprise and she had replied to their questions without thinking. For the rest they had written up the article out of their imagination.

(It was, however, partly on account of the Shyira incident that I was later awarded the Royal African Society's medal, 'For dedicated service to Africa.' I received it at the same time as Dr. Helen Roseveare of Congo fame, and Dr. Stanley Brown, the leprologist responsible for the breakthrough in leprosy treatment.)

Shortly after these events in Rwanda I was sent to Buye in Burundi to be Education Secretary for the Anglican Church in both countries. This role involved more heavy office work, handling school accounts and ordering supplies for all the schools, distributing these as well as the teachers' salaries. Much time was spent travelling the length and breadth of the two countries (between which there was no frontier until Independence), in very unsettled conditions, and often with enormous sums of money, to pay the teachers, in the boot of my car! Most of the early '60s continued to be times of unrest; we had to carry passes wherever we went, and there were armed check-points at every road junction. Looking back on these journeys I marvel at God's protection of me, and give heartfelt thanks to the friends praying in England who upheld us in those dangerous days. Again and again, as I had to pass through the armed check-points I experienced a special sense of the peace of God, whether alone or with African passengers, some of whom did not have road passes or were wanting to escape from Rwanda. I shall never forget the gratitude in the eyes of one old former chief, David. As we crossed the border into Burundi he turned to me and said, 'You have saved me from the mouth of the lion!' Once as I drew up to a barrier where other cars were being searched, one of the soldiers called out, 'Oh, it's Mademoiselle Peck! She used to teach me. Open the barrier for her!' Another time, a group of soldiers gathered round the car window, to the alarm of my passenger, a visitor from Europe, who thought they were going to shoot us. A soldier leaned in and said, 'Please, have you got a hymnbook we could have? We get so bored here and would like to sing some hymns.'

But the most amazing time I thank God for was when the situation was very tense prior to Independence, and all cars were being searched for arms. As I stopped the car, I was ordered, 'Come on out, give us your gun!'

'I haven't got one,' I replied.

'Oh yes you have,' they insisted. 'All white people carry guns.'

'Look,' I said, 'I have come to Rwanda to share the Good News of God's love in Jesus Christ. What would I want with a gun?'

'No, of course not,' they reluctantly agreed, and lifted the barrier to wave me through!

Although political disturbances were by now widespread, the Belgian Administration were reluctant to step in and prevent what was going on, for those creating the tension were the majority ethnic group, and as a United Nations Trustee country, Belgium could not be seen to be opposing democratic movements. In that climate of escalating tribal feeling it was difficult to remain impartial; impossible to act, or not to act, without appearing to take sides.

However, apparent lack of government support for them angered the Tutsi chiefs, who were still nominally in their old jobs. They felt they had been let down by those they served. They went, en masse, to the authorities to resign, and their resignation was accepted.

On 1st July, 1962, Independence was granted to Rwanda and Burundi. (When the Congo had received its Independence from Belgium, Rwandans had been up in arms, literally and metaphorically: 'What! Those pagan Congolese, no better than cannibals, granted Independence before us!') In January the previous year a Republican Government had been declared, and in September a plebiscite held, under the auspices of the United Nations, for the people to decide on the status of the King and whether they wished to continue with the monarchical or republican system. They chose the latter, though we heard that a great deal of intimidation took place at the polling booths (the UN officials could not be everywhere).

Despite the fact that a majority Hutu government had been established, numbers of Tutsi stayed on in Rwanda, particularly those in leadership in the churches and many ordinary church members. 'If we leave,' they said, 'how can the testimony continue of Christ making us one across the ethnic divisions?' Nevertheless, large numbers of Tutsi did leave (as well as the thousands who had fled the violence of 1959-60), crossing over into the Congo, Burundi, Tanzania and, most importantly, Uganda. The King, who had been refused re-entry into the country even prior to Independence, while on a visit to the Congo for their Independence celebrations, fled to Kenya and later settled in the USA.

Refugees now played an increasingly large part in my own life, too, as well as in the affairs of the nation. In the course of my educational work I found myself making frequent visits to the large refugee camp at Nyamata, setting up classes for the children there and in the district around as groups of refugees began to resettle on smallholdings throughout the area. Nyamata was situated in the south-eastern part of Rwanda known as the Bugesera, once a separate kingdom but annexed by Rwandan kings in the 16th century and used as a place of exile for their enemies. For years a neglected inhospitable place of swamps, crocodile-infested rivers, long savannah grass and thorn trees - home to the sleeping-sickness tsetse fly and herds of wild buffalo - with only a few scattered settlements, the land had, from the mid-1950s, been sprayed regularly to help control the tsetse fly, some marshes drained and roads built to open up the area for development. A land ready for receiving thousands of people!

Ruhorohoza, the chief, was a Protestant - in fact, the only 'full' chief who ever became one. He was still in residence when I first started visiting and planning new schools, and was always most hospitable and helpful in granting us any sites we wanted for churches and schools.

The refugee camps centred around the small trading post and RC out-school at Nyamata. People were housed in makeshift shelters, whole families being crowded into one room 6ft. by 6ft. They cooked the small rations they were given over open fires, and an atmosphere of despair pervaded the camps. The refugees were revising the old proverb, 'God spends the day elsewhere, but comes home to Rwanda at night.' They were now saying, 'He has forgotten the way home to us.' Quite soon, however, a team of RC and Protestant volunteers led by Monsieur Triplot, a very dedicated and resourceful Belgian administrator, undertook the task of encouraging the refugees to resettle on smallholdings in the district around. It was a difficult task as they had, naturally enough, what is called the 'refugee mentality', that is, a fixed idea that they will be returning to their own land soon, so are opposed to the suggestion that they make a permanent settlement in the land of exile. Then one day, as I returned from a trip to Burundi, I was met by Monsieur Triplot: 'Mademoiselle,' he said, ' this is the best day of my life! The refugees have agreed to being resettled!' So gradually the moving out took place, from the discomfort of the overcrowded camp, on to their own plots of land where they could cultivate food for themselves - though the majority of them being cattle people they had at first little experience of agriculture. They were given materials to help them build and roof their houses, with corrugated tin sheeting. And eventually, in accordance with the government policy of integration, they became known as 'abaturage' (that is, residents), rather than 'impunzi' (refugees).

The afternoon before Independence I drove back into Rwanda from making another visit to Urundi, for the last time. From now on we would have to reside definitely in one country or the other; constant crossing and re-crossing of the border would no longer be so easy. It had been decided that I would live in Rwanda, and as my main work was with the new settlements, a house had been built for me at Maranyundo, the developing

Anglican church centre near Nyamata. On my journey back I met several cars with former mission workers of other Protestant missions, leaving the country. They were surprised that I was returning as there was a widespread feeling that more trouble would break out in Rwanda. My house had been built fairly near to that of the Rwandan pastor, Yona Kanamuzeyi - he and his wife Mary and their children were already firm friends of mine. Some time later Yona told me that he had not slept that night before Independence, but had spent the night patrolling around my house. He had not been concerned that I would experience any trouble from the Africans, but was a little anxious about the group of Belgian soldiers stationed nearby. The thought of trouble from any quarter had not entered my head, and I slept happily in my new home.

Together with members of the local Christian community and their pastor, James Kayinamura, Yona and I supervised the distribution of vast quantities of relief supplies - clothing, food, medicines, etc, sent by various relief organisations, including Oxfam, Inter-Church Aid (later renamed Christian Aid), and Bread for the World, who as well as supplying seed for planting, sent us a Do It Yourself temporary school building kit! All the pieces were numbered, and in accordance with the diagram we were able to put up a nice sized building which served many purposes. Much time was spent preaching and teaching, and establishing out-schools over the resettlement area. Eventually we were able to fire bricks in our own kiln and start the building of a large brick church on Maranyundo site itself - whereas previously the large services had been held in the open air with just a temporary sheltered platform for the speakers. Large numbers of people attended the services, and many came to a living faith in Jesus Christ as their Lord and Saviour. One ex-chief from the Kigeme area came to me one day saying he wanted to share his story with me. 'Many years ago,' he began, 'when the Spirit of God was moving in your churches, I used to hear this message and felt a strong prompting in my heart to respond. But at that time the Protestant faith was not very well looked upon in official circles, and I heard that the King discouraged chiefs from joining. I thought to myself, if I respond and become known as a Protestant I may lose my job, my house, my cows - how would I and my family live? So I shut my ears to this inner voice. Then the Revolution broke out. I lost my job, my house, my cattle, and arrived here with nothing except my shorts and shirt - oh, and a tie! Then again I heard you people singing and preaching, and once again felt the prompting in my heart. This time I responded.' Then he added, 'I look around me now and I see my family and I are all clothed, we eat adequately, I have a house and land where I am discovering that you can dig in the ground, plant seeds and they grow! So here I am, with all that I need and with a priceless peace in my heart.'

Another much older man, who had been a chief since the Germans had first settled the country, had come to the refugee camp already a Christian of many years standing, but also having lost everything. One day he said to me, 'I have served under four kings and there is not an evil thing I have not done, even murder, but now I serve the King of Kings, and I know that my sins have all been cleansed in the Blood of Jesus.'

As time went on and people cultivated their gardens, we saw a wilderness begin to blossom. I made frequent journeys to a nearby Agricultural Research centre further south in the Bugesera, and brought back fruit trees and bushes for planting. Then from our own Mission's 'Christian Rural Service' project based at Shyogwe, I was able to obtain and distribute Rhode Island Red cockerels to improve the standard of local poultry, which although resistant to endemic diseases were small and produced few and very small eggs.

Camping at Nyamata; Yona Kanamuzeyi on the right

While in the Bugesera we felt a sense of renewed hope, on the wider scene there were still tensions. Groups of Tutsi exiles (known as 'inyenzi', or cockroaches) began to make raids over the borders in their attempts to regain a footing in what they regarded as their home. This fomented fear and mistrust among some Hutu leaders in the government towards the Tutsi still in the country, although many of them had accepted the new regime and were working together with the Hutu to rebuild the life of the country.

Towards the end of 1963 I returned to England for home leave, so was not at Maranyundo when rumours of an invasion by armed refugees from Burundi threatened the stability of the Bugesera and, in particular, of Nyamata, which lay on the invasion route to Kigali. The attempt was thwarted by the Burundi government forces who captured some of the leaders and seized two lorries full of weapons.

But in December a second force broke through. Passing through Nyamata they pushed on to Kigali, where they suffered defeat by the Rwandan army. Proven supporters of the invasion were arrested and executed. Suspected sympathisers were hunted out, imprisoned or murdered. Finally, the hunt extended to others of Tutsi extraction. In some areas, particularly around Kigeme, wholesale massacres took place.

The invading force had not left the Bugesera area unaffected. Soldiers were posted nearby and arrests and killings occurred during weeks of terror. Towards the end of January, Pastor Yona, seen as a Tutsi (though like many in Rwanda he was of mixed tribal descent) and because of his work among the Tutsi refugees, was arrested by a group of soldiers one night, who said they wanted to question him. I heard later that he had been allowed time to comfort Mary and the children, assuring them he would return soon - but he and Mary both knew what a night-time visit from soldiers meant. Knowing the risk he ran even though he had not involved himself in politics and had constantly exhorted the local settlers to have nothing to do with the extremists, Yona had persistently refused to leave the area, taking refuge only in his faith in God, believing that he should stay with the flock he loved and felt called to care for.

He was taken off in an army jeep, along with the headmaster of the local primary school and one other man, and driven to the river crossing on the way to Kigali, stopping on the further side of the river where they were met by more soldiers. One of them said, 'You had better pray to your God.' So Yona prayed: 'Lord God, you know that we have not sinned against the Government, and now I pray you look upon our innocent blood and help these men who know not what they are doing. In the Name of Jesus Christ our Lord. Amen.'

Andrew, the schoolmaster, was set free, but warned not to tell anyone what had happened. Yona was then led back to the river bridge. Before many minutes had passed a shot rang out. Yona's body was thrown into the river.

It was reported that Yona had walked to his execution singing a hymn, like a carefree man going to meet his father, trusting in the God who had saved him, who had kept him on his path, who had used him greatly in the extending of his kingdom, and who now called him home to be with him.

If you visit St. Paul's Cathedral in London, you will see Yona's name among the list of modern martyrs in the Memorial Chapel, the chapel which commemorates those who, in the last 150 years, have 'witnessed to Christ and suffered death rather than renounce Him.'

Chapter 7
Renewal

At the time Yona was murdered I was still on leave in England. I received the news by letter from the Ruanda Mission office while at home in Reigate. I was numbed, and felt somehow guilty that I had left Maranyundo, as I doubted Yona would have been taken off and shot had I still been there. The next day the General Secretary of the Mission, Rev. John Collinson, rang me to give me the opportunity to talk about it; his sensitive understanding helped me enormously in being able to look forward again with renewed hope.

These few months on home service took me a stage further in my spiritual learning as I actually began to experience for myself at last what I had encountered theoretically during my time in Belgium among the Pentecostal fellowships there. This new dimension in spiritual experience began during a stay with the Lee Abbey Community in North Devon, where a friend of mine from Reigate, Christine Macnair, a former CIM (China Inland Mission, now Overseas Missionary Fellowship) missionary in China, was now a Deaconness. After I had had a chance to relax on the beautiful Devon coast, she said she 'felt led' to enlighten me about how the Holy Spirit was moving in the Western Church scene, particularly in the United States. 'Doreen,' she said, 'you've come home from several years in the remote parts of Africa, and I think you need to be aware of what God is doing in the churches, in what people are calling "Charismatic Renewal".' She gave me a book to read, *Speaking in Tongues: A Gift for the Body of Christ* by Larry Christensen, which introduced some aspects of this 'renewal'. I was somewhat surprised that she would be interested in such a movement, as I had thought of her hitherto as a stolid fundamentalist evangelical. So, after reading the book, which revived memories of all my ponderings in Belgium, I asked her, 'What do you know personally, Christine, of the "gifts of the Spirit" which this book speaks about?' She replied, 'I can only share my testimony of what happened to me.' Very simply, a clergy friend had been praying with her for a fresh empowering of the Holy Spirit for her ministry at Lee Abbey when she became conscious of an inner release and deep joy, and began to speak 'in tongues'. She went on to say that she felt she had been given new insights into the Word of God, and a deeper discernment in her ministry.

I took this book with me to read again on the cliff-top near Lee Abbey. As I prayed over what I was reading, I was struck by one particular sentence, in the section where the author speaks of receiving God's gifts for spiritual warfare. For some years I had prayed, 'Lord, if you see that I have need of any of these "gifts of the Spirit", please give me what it is that I need.' But Christensen pointed out that we are not told to pray like that when seeking the gift of salvation; we are told simply to say, 'Lord, save me!' and accept by faith that He has done so. In the same way, he points out, with regard to the gifts of the Spirit, which are clearly mentioned in Scripture, we should ask for them and accept by faith that He has given them to us, saying, 'Thank you, Lord, for your gift.' The gifts are not, after all, for our own benefit but for the benefit of others - for example, the gift of healing is for the sick person; we are channels only of the Spirit's gifts.

All this stayed very much in my thoughts as I returned to my deputation programme, speaking at churches and meetings across the country, and including a visit to Brussels to renew contacts made during my year's residence there, but especially to share in a special meeting about the ministry of the Mission in Rwanda, Burundi and Uganda.

My father had died while I was in Burundi in 1961; he was killed in a train accident just outside Redhill station as he was returning from ringing the bells at St. Paul's Cathedral. He was 78 years old and still very fit, and I know he would have been grateful for such a sudden end to earthly life whilst still involved in doing what he most enjoyed. In fact, he had said to me that he was determined to keep active and involved with life as long as possible. 'I cannot contemplate getting to the stage of some old folk I see, sitting on the seat at the corner of the road, just doing nothing but watch the traffic go by!' A memorial service was held for him in Westminster Abbey, but to my great regret I wasn't able to be there as it wasn't possible in those days to get back quickly from Burundi.

Now, while I was home in England my sister and family shared with me the need they felt to move to Crawley to be nearer Patrick's work, which meant they wished to sell the family home and use their share for a house in Crawley. Some Reigate friends offered to store for me any pieces of furniture or other articles I especially wanted to keep from my old home; meanwhile I went to stay with an old school friend in Reigate while continuing local deputation meetings. While staying there I had time alone to think over again what I had learned from my Lee Abbey experience and reading. One day, during a special time of quiet and prayer, I asked the Lord for the gift of tongues, praying, 'Thank you, Lord, for this gift.' I asked for the gift of tongues because this particular gift seemed at that time to be the distinguishing sign between the mainline Christians and those classified as Charismatic. I opened my mouth and some syllables formed. Was this 'tongues', I wondered? Or my own efforts? I wasn't sure.

That evening I was due to speak at an evening meeting at St. Mary's, Reigate, whose CMS Link Missionary I was. And, contrary to my normal sense of diffidence in that rather erudite gathering, I felt a new freedom as I spoke. Some time afterwards my friend's husband wrote to me, and made a comment about 'the meeting at which you spoke so powerfully' - not a comment anyone had ever made about me before!

Having returned to Rwanda I was immediately caught up in my work as 'Inspectrice', based first at Shyogwe where Bert Osborn had established the Diocesan Education Office, and later at Kigeme. The independent Rwandan Government had decided to administer the country's schools through recognised Inspectors for the various denominations. I was appointed the Government Inspector for the Anglican primary schools. This involved travelling round the country inspecting, equipping and encouraging the work being done by the (by now) hundreds of schoolteachers. It also meant writing reports, submitting requests for new classes, and seeing to the distribution of teachers' salaries each month. In this work I was fortunate to have the assistance of an able accountant, a former student at Shyogwe College, Modeste Mudaheranwa who later succeeded me as Inspector.

It was this travelling role that meant my having to move from the refugee resettlement centre at Nyamata where I had worked with such harmony with Pastor Yona. His murder at the beginning of 1964 had overwhelmed all who had known him, and even those not connected with the Anglican Church were grieved at his untimely death. 'Why,' people asked, 'had he been taken when he had been such a power for good?' Answers were discovered in comparing the present situation with the history of the early Church, that through his death the message and power of forgiveness might reach others. Like the first martyr Stephen, Yona had died praying for forgiveness for those murdering him. As the death of Stephen had its effect on Paul, so the manner of Yona's dying had its effect on many. The Rwandan church recognised it was living through times of testing similar to those of the early persecuted church, and they responded in the same way. They rejoiced that they were counted worthy to suffer for the Name of Jesus. Outstanding among testimonies at this time was that of Mary, Yona's widow. She wrote to a friend, 'For my part I want you to know that Jesus has been very near to me. At first after Yona had gone, I fell into days of despair. But then the Lord Jesus gave me this word from Mark 9:8, *"And suddenly when they looked round about, they saw no man any more save Jesus only."* And he reminded me of Hymn 362 in our book: 'Jesus is mine'. It is true that Jesus is mine; even though I have lost the friend whose life I shared and with whom I used to talk everything over, yet - Jesus is mine!'

God answered the needs and prayers of the church in the refugee resettlement area by sending one of Yona's close friends, Eustace Kajuga, who with his wife Marianne had trained with Yona and Mary at Buye and had been ordained with him in 1960. I had the great joy of introducing him to the several thousand Christians still at Maranyundo, the Anglican Church centre at Nyamata, following his unanimous appointment there by the Diocesan Committee in July 1964. Towards the end of the year he wrote, 'Here in the Bugesera we are well. We have many new people who have begun to learn [i.e. Christian teaching] and among them some have been saved. We have many children in our schools and many young girls come to the Girls' Club to learn useful skills as well as elements of the Christian faith. There is a teacher who helps Marianne; but what worries us most is that most of the children have no decent clothes - but we see that Jesus holds us in his hand and satisfies us.'

By this time (December 1964) I had been asked to move to Kigeme - the reason being a shortage of missionary medical personnel. When the resident doctor had gone on leave there was no doctor to replace him; the Sister in charge, Rosemary Preston, agreed to stay on without a resident doctor, and such was the confidence which people had in our nursing sisters that the hospital remained full and the clinics continued to draw large numbers. Her courage, her cheerfulness and tireless efforts meant a very great deal to the Kigeme people, but finally her own leave was due - hence my arrival! I was the only missionary available with a car to go there and enable the hospital to continue functioning adequately. I had to be on call to ferry urgent cases with which the African staff could not cope, taking them in my car to the nearest doctor, twenty-five miles away; see to the ordering and collecting of drugs from Kigali; keep records up to date; and be responsible for the pastoral oversight of the staff, sharing in Christian fellowship with them.

Derelict houses, overgrown gardens, empty classrooms, a doctorless hospital, fatherless children, widows with sad faces and tragic memories. Such was my impression as I moved in. An 'earth-bound' view indeed, yet quite a useful basis for an account of the events that year at Kigeme - surely the most difficult since the work began there in 1932.

The fresh outbreak of violence in early 1964 was nowhere more terrible than in that area. Several school, hospital and church workers, as well as many ordinary church members, were killed; others fled, thus leaving sad gaps in every department, and empty houses all around. Lack of certificated teachers meant we could not open the first year of another boys' secondary school like the one at Shyogwe. Thirty-six local boys were unable to continue their education though they had passed the government entrance examination for secondary schools. This resulted in several empty school buildings and, more important, feelings of frustration in the hearts of these boys and their families, and apprehension among pupils still in primary school that when their turn came there would be no places for them.

However, I had not been at Kigeme long before I realised how misleading my first impressions had been. As I talked with one person and another I found a deep confidence that the Lord still had a purpose to fulfil here and that, though many had poignant memories, they were looking forward not back. The hospital staff, under the leadership of Simeon Ngiringubu, were determined that standards of hygiene and efficiency should not slip. Patients were well cared for and their spiritual needs not neglected. Simeon wrote for the Friends of Ruanda Annual Report about these times: 'Although we have been without a doctor or sister, the Lord Jesus has been with us. He has guided us and given us wisdom that in ourselves we do not possess. So we have been able to carry on the work of caring for the sick.... We know that God will not let us down.....'

Although buildings stood empty, I found that there were more children than ever attending the ordinary primary church schools - over 200 on the Mission Centre and some 6,000 in the rest of the Kigeme church area. I asked the local school Director what he felt was especially of note that year, and he answered, 'The interest the children seem to be showing these days in spiritual things. We have recently started a special service in church each Wednesday morning and the children look forward to it, and discuss it in a way I have not seen for several years.' I myself found as I visited different churches in the area that much larger numbers were attending the various Sunday schools.

As the only white person for twenty-five miles, and the only Mission Partner for very much further, I found more precious than ever the fellowship and loving concern of the Christian fellowship, and especially that of Archdeacon Festo Gakware and his wife Julina. At this time Festo wrote the following message for the Friends of Ruanda Annual Report: 'I am so glad to be able to send our greetings and to tell you how we are these days, so that you may know how to pray and believe for us. We have passed through times of great testing.... I do want to make it clear, however, and for this we do praise God so much, that His work here is going ahead. Perhaps you have imagined that all the troubles you have read about have put an end to it? By no means! There are still many, many people left in our churches, and more are joining us all the time. Last month I baptised 150 adults.... We have 15,639 church members and another 2,457 waiting for baptism. In the beginners' instruction classes there are at present 9,867. So you see how God is answering your prayers. Of course we do have problems and difficulties, and are sometimes assailed by fears. But on the cover of my radio set, I have printed the following text: *'Be of good cheer; I have overcome the world.'* Sometimes when I listen to the news of the wars and other evils of our sick world, I begin to get downhearted and worried, then as I shut down the cover of the set I see those words and am helped to "lift my eyes" and see Him who overcame on the Cross - and peace returns. He is the only remedy for all our sicknesses, and His kingdom of peace is surely drawing near!'

Both Festo and Simeon have already passed into the Lord's unclouded presence, but the confidence of faith which their words portray is still present in the truly born-again church members, as was evidenced again and again in the testimonies of many, both young and old, during more recent years following the genocide of 1994 and its aftermath.

During this time as the only white face at Kigeme, I was very aware of the Lord's providence and protection, especially as I made night-time trips down the steep road to the government hospital at Astrida (Butare), with women patients in difficult labour whom our own hospital staff felt needed more expert help than they could give. I made the mistake on the first of these journeys of seating the patient in the front seat next to me. As her pains increased she started thrashing around and flung her arm across my face, so that I narrowly missed swerving down a precipice! After that I always sat the patient in the back seat with a hospital worker.

Soon after Rosemary returned from leave we had another example of the Lord's omnipotent care. Some years previously a Belgian benevolent fund (funded by their National Lottery!) had installed electric generators and water pumps in centres of population where there was a hospital or boarding school. This was a tremendous help of course, as it meant that work, even operations, could be carried out at night without the chore of lighting and trimming oil lamps, and obviously giving much better lighting. But, when the system went wrong there was no skilled person available to put it right. One evening as dusk was falling the man responsible for switching on the electric generator knocked on my door to tell me it would not function. Rosemary was away for the night, and a visit to the engine-house myself brought no better result. Dusty storm-lanterns and pressure-lamps were unearthed, and anyone having a store of paraffin shared it around. The odd candle was produced, and people managed somehow. Mercifully there were no emergencies in the hospital that night.

Next morning as I knelt to pray I read in my daily Bible reading passage from Philippians 4:6-7 (I was using J. B. Phillips' *Letters to Young Churches*, one of the first of the modern English translations) - *'Don't worry about anything whatever; tell God every detail of your needs in earnest and thankful prayer, and the peace of God which transcends human understanding, will keep constant guard over your hearts and minds as they rest in Christ Jesus.'*

'All right, Lord,' I said. 'I need an electrician!'

That day I was due to collect some school supplies from Kigali, several hours' drive away, so as I passed through our nearest town, Astrida, I called in on one of the Asian shop-keepers whom I knew well and asked him if there was an electrician anywhere around. 'No,' he said. 'There was one travelling round the Roman Catholic Mission centres installing generators, but he has recently left again for Europe. There isn't another in the whole country.' We continued our journey along the main road towards Kigali (Archdeacon Festo was with me). After some miles we saw a young white man standing by the roadside thumbing us down. I stopped and he asked, in French, for a lift to Kigali, explaining that he needed to go there to finalise arrangements for his luggage and his journey home. I noticed he spoke French with a slight accent. When he saw on my dashboard a little praise chorus in German (given me by Corrie ten Boom) his face lit up. 'German!' he exclaimed. 'I am German.'

'What have you been doing in Rwanda?' I asked.

'I'm an electrician,' he replied. 'I've been installing generators in the Roman Catholic Missions.'

I almost gasped in unbelief! And recounted to him our plight at Kigeme. After listening to my story he simply said, 'I shall have to come and help, shan't I? Where is this place?' When I told him it was fifty kilometres behind us, he suggested a place where I might pick him up just outside Kigali the following morning to give him a lift to the hospital. He had just that one day left before catching his plane home.

He spent the whole day examining and repairing the entire network of wiring and other parts, and refused any payment for all his trouble and expertise in mending the generator. The next morning I took him down to the main road where he hitched a lift back to catch his plane for Europe. I still marvel that the one qualified electrician in a country the size of Wales should have been standing on the busy main road I was driving along, and it should have been my car that he thumbed down! *Tell God every detail of your needs!* For all the years I was at Kigeme there was never any trouble with the generator after that.

The empty school buildings at one end of the Kigeme hill, which in my earlier years there had been the centre of a flourishing Girls' Boarding School, set me dreaming of re-establishing something similar. There were so many girls, some of them daughters of senior church workers, who had no hope of further education yet had great potential. To my joy, several of the local church leaders and a former teacher who was now an MP had the same vision. But we had no resources, and the Minister of Education had decreed that there would be no more subsidised classes for a year. We prayed and planned, nevertheless, and our MP friend talked to the Minister of Education, who as a result agreed to make us an exception! So we could start a class for post-primary students for teacher-training and general studies at the commencement of the school year. I had the help of Claudette, a gifted girl teacher, and Christopher, a school manager and teacher of long experience. Others rallied round and we tidied up buildings that had fallen into disrepair, made new desks, beds, and other equipment, and I began recruiting pupils from the Sixth forms of all the denominations, including some Roman Catholics. Some had been expelled from one of the other Protestant Mission schools for too many 'order marks' received, and which inside knowledge led me to feel were for too trivial offences. At the beginning of the term I gathered them all together to explain our ethos, as responsible students training to lead others. 'There will be no rules here,' I said, 'except that staff must be obeyed without demur, and no-one may visit the "dukas" [the shops at the local trading-post] without permission.'

'What, no order marks?' they gasped incredulously.

'No order marks,' I confirmed.

For that whole year that I was in charge we had no disciplinary problems whatsoever. In subsequent years the school grew encouragingly under the leadership of Mabel Jones, Jean Dabinett, Jennifer Noyelle and Lilette Honoré. It developed eventually into a mixed establishment of high educational repute.

One of the joys of my role as Schools Inspector was to travel round the country and meet up with colleagues in various places. I discovered that some of them had been experiencing, as I had during my home leave, a fresh realisation of the empowering of the Holy Spirit. Some had received gifts of the Spirit, and we shared what we had learned, encouraging one another to be open to God in new ways. Then on a brief visit to Kampala for dental treatment (the nearest dentist at that time!) I was able to link up again with Corrie ten Boom and her secretary/companion Connie von Hoogstraten (later Hogerzeil).

Corrie, the Dutch evangelist who had been incarcerated by the Nazis in Ravensbruck for helping Jews escape from Holland, had previously visited Rwanda and Burundi, sharing her story of her forgiveness of those prison guards who had ill-treated her, and under whom her father and sister had died. That visit was just prior to the revolution of 1959-60 in Rwanda, and after the turmoil of those days many people who had suffered gave testimony to how much Corrie's words had helped them to forgive and to be reconciled with those who had wronged them. I had met Corrie and Connie at that time. Now they were spending time in Uganda, as the Lord had told Corrie that if she had a year's rest from travelling and speaking he would give her another ten years in world ministry. The year was nearly up, and she felt another visit to Rwanda would be the right thing just now. One day she and I were walking quietly by the shore of one of the inlets of Lake Victoria when she began to share with me the fresh experience of the Holy Spirit's anointing that she had received some years previously. She spoke of receiving spiritual gifts, particularly the gift of 'tongues', and the difference she felt this had made to her ministry. I was amazed that she should share this with me, and more so when she told me I was the first person in Africa that she had mentioned it to, but that she'd felt the Lord's leading to do so. I then told her how the Lord had been opening up these truths to me also, but that I doubted whether the 'words' I had uttered was truly the gift of tongues. She began to pray in tongues there and then, and I was able to join in. From that time on I used this form of prayer whenever I was uncertain of how to pray for a particular situation, or if I felt confused or under stress, and found I began to have a deep sense of peace.

When Corrie made her second Rwanda-Burundi journey I was able to accompany her for much of it, acting as her interpreter. As she found our roads too bumpy and uncomfortable for her 'ageing bones', she hired a small plane, usually from Missionary Aviation Fellowship, and we flew from centre to centre. She would use vivid visual illustrations for her stories, and over the period of time I became very familiar with the anecdotes and the teaching she drew from them. One day she was not feeling at all well, so we met to discuss plans. 'Never mind,' she said, 'Doreen knows all I say by heart. She can take the meeting!' However, Connie and I laid hands on her and prayed for restoration of strength. Much to my relief, she got up happily and was able to take the meeting!

Several of Corrie's sayings have long stayed with me. She used to challenge people who used the phrase 'under the circumstances' - as Christians we ought not to say or think that: 'we are *over* them, for we are in Christ and He reigns!' Another comment was that we must avoid 'a worm's eye view' - and take rather 'a bird's eye view'! And in perplexing situations she would say, 'God has no problems, only plans.' Often when sharing the Gospel message she would say (referring to Micah 7:19), 'God has cast all our sins in the depth of the sea,' - then add, 'and has put up a notice NO FISHING!' She had postcards printed in Holland depicting a cross standing in the midst of choppy waters, with the words on the cross 'Verboden te vissen!' ('Fishing forbidden!') I still keep in my Bible my copy of this postcard from Corrie.

For her own living expenses Corrie used her Dutch old-age pension, but for all the other needs of her worldwide ministry she lived 'by faith'. When some particular need arose for which she did not have the resources she would say, 'Lord, all the cattle on a thousand hills are yours. Couldn't you just sell one cow for this need?' And the money would come in!

Corrie had a very well-respected ministry in the USA and she spoke a great deal to me about how the Lord was bringing spiritual renewal to the churches in North America, not merely in Pentecostal circles but in the Episcopal Church as well. 'Why don't you go and stay in America and experience what God is doing in some of the churches there?' she suggested. 'I can't just go and stay like that!' I replied. 'Yes, you can - Harriet would love to have you.' Harriet being one of the special friends Corrie mentioned often, and her home being where she normally made her base when visiting the States.

Meanwhile, we discussed what the Bible speaks of as the 'baptism in the Holy Spirit', about which I had been reading and praying for so long. Believing that I had received the Holy Spirit at conversion and that I had already asked for and trusted that I had received the filling of the Spirit 'by faith', I was hesitant at the thought of seeking 'experiences'. However, one day, alone in my room at Kigeme, I knelt and prayed again that the Holy Spirit would search my heart and show me any hindrance to a fresh infilling of God's Spirit. For some time I had been conscious of inhibitions and attitudes that seemed to bind me from true liberty in ministry, and thinking back over my early years I felt that I was still affected by my mother's treating me as the boy she had longed for, calling me 'my Basil' and making me feel that it was second-rate to be a girl. Other influences from a rather Victorian-style upbringing ('Children should be seen and not heard') had, I felt, given me an inferiority complex. It seemed that much from my subconscious was still affecting my present attitudes and behaviour.

As I continued in quiet prayer, a verse from Hebrews (4:12) came clearly into my mind: *'The word of God is living and active, sharper than any two-edged sword, piercing to the division of soul and spirit, of joints and marrow, and discerning the thoughts and intentions of the heart.'* 'Lord,' I prayed, 'where is it that soul and spirit meet?' And I felt that he told me, 'the subconscious.'

'Then let the Holy Spirit pierce right down to that place, and expose and heal those hidden hurts, that old conditioning from my early experiences,' I prayed.

Spiritual experiences are hard to express in words, but I knew that a cleansing, healing wave was indeed sweeping through my inner being, bringing peace. Then came an amazing sense of the Lord's love flowing over and over me, and a joy filled my heart so that it seemed it would burst. Eventually I cried, 'Lord, I can't take any more!' What should I call such an experience? The baptism in the Holy Spirit? Certainly it was the beginning of a new dimension of Christian living. Bishop Simon Barrington-Ward, a former General Secretary of CMS and former Bishop of Coventry, used the term 'immersed in the Spirit', and that expresses it so well for me. An illustration he once gave was of a shell at the edge of the sea, filled with water from the sea after the tide had washed over it, then of the shell being plunged into the sea as the waves sweep over it again.

This deeper appreciation of God's illimitable Spirit was a very timely preparation for some of the journeys I took with Corrie ten Boom to parts of the country where many pre-Christian practices still held sway. People consulted spiritual 'healers' and joined in some of the old ritual 'rites of passage'. They feared the influences of the ancestors and other spirits, making offerings to them. Corrie was very sensitive to oppressive forces and would say, 'I feel there is witchcraft around, or other influences of the powers of darkness.' Often in a meeting she would ask the congregation if they felt truly free in spirit, or whether they sometimes wanted to pray in public, or give a testimony, or indeed respond to a Gospel appeal, but somehow felt bound and could not. 'If that is the case,' she would ask, 'is it that you have been involved in some occult practice, or consulted local soothsayers or healers?' Each time she asked such questions, Christians - sometimes those of long-standing - would come up to her and say that they did sense this spiritual 'bondage'. After finding out what involvement they had had with these occult practices, she would cut them off from their spiritual influence, claiming freedom in the Name of Jesus. Their joy was often wonderful to see! Corrie told me she found this spiritual bondage was common in Europe also, and that there were influences that came from such things as astrology, ouija boards (very popular at that time), and Freemasonry.

Listening to Corrie, I was conscious that I too experienced a hesitation, which I often gave in to, when I wanted to share in open prayer or give a testimony. I told her of my close involvement with my father's Freemasonry, how I used to help him learn certain passages for meetings or clean his masonic regalia. She prayed for me, cutting me off from any remaining influence from this.

However, from time to time I was aware that there was still some lingering bondage of spirit, particularly during times of great blessing and power in a meeting or time of worship. I was made aware of this again at a conference in England some time later, when there was a wonderful moving of the Holy Spirit with deep praise, worship and ministry for healing. One of those leading the conference was Edgar Trout, a leader in the Renewal movement in the late '60s, who spoke about the various occult practices that could cause spiritual bondage. I remembered then very clearly how, when on holiday in Germany with a group of my sister's

Ranger friends, we had been introduced to the ouija board. We sat round a table with letters of the alphabet circling it and our fingers on an upturned wineglass. One of the girls who had used the board before asked, 'Who is the medium among us?' The wineglass started to move around the table, though it did not feel as though anyone was pushing it, and to my amazement spelt out the letters of my name! After that we asked other questions and received answers that we could not have known ourselves. Even so, I did not really take it seriously, though when I returned to school I told some of my friends about it and we thought it would be fun to have a go. We did this once or twice until one day I asked if there was a special message for anyone, and when the reply came that it was for me, with the words, 'Work always for Jesus,' I sensed somehow a subtle snare. It seemed incongruous that the name of Jesus should be associated with this, as I was starting to understand that it verged on spiritualism, so I got up from the table and would never touch it again. Later I heard that some of my Crusader friends had been praying about my involvement with the practice.

So, at the Renewal conference I decided to talk to Edgar Trout about this involvement with ouija boards. He was very clear that I needed deliverance from its influence, even though it had taken place so many years before. He prayed with great authority and cut me off from it all, and I became conscious of a deep release and new freedom of spirit. This episode underlined for me the fact that one must not be naive about the negative and hampering effect on the spirit that such occult forces can exercise on Christian lives and ministry. Since then there have been occasions when I have been given a spirit of discernment that there were occult or demonic influences involved and that certain places or people needed to be set free by the authority of the Name of Jesus. Even Christians, in these so-called modern (or should one say post-modern?) days, can be unaware of the fact, or even discount, that an important aspect of the Christian faith is the battle against satanic powers, that hinder the free moving of the Holy Spirit and attempt to blind or ensnare us, be it through spiritualism, witchcraft, or occult forces in whatever cultural context they appear.

While Corrie ten Boom was staying with us at Kigeme, a student from Shyogwe College was sent to the hospital at Kigeme as he was behaving very strangely and was thought to be schizophrenic. Quite a gifted student academically, he had suddenly taken on the personality of an old man. It was realised that this had begun after he had been playing such a part in a French play at school in the course of which he had had to say, 'J'ai donné mon coeur au diable' ('I have given my soul to the devil') - and it was as if he had been taken over by this other personality. Knowing about this I asked Corrie if she would meet with him. When he entered the house she felt straightaway that this was a case of demonic influence, even possession, especially as the drugs he had been given had made no improvement in his condition. She asked Connie and two other Christians to sit nearby and pray while she and I sat with the boy (I was interpreting for her). First she encouraged him, with some firmness, to look her straight in the eyes, which took some time to achieve, then she commanded the demonic spirit that was troubling the boy to come out 'in the Name of Jesus' and to go where Jesus commanded and not to enter anyone else. Immediately the boy shook himself, stood up and said, 'Oh, where am I? I feel so different!' Then putting his hand in his pocket he pulled out a small ornament that had been on a shelf in our house, saying, 'Look, this is what I took from you as I came in' - we had not noticed him doing this - 'and I've more things that I stole from the hospital. Somehow I had no control over my actions.' He returned to college and finished his training, and as long as we were in touch with him he behaved perfectly normally. When speaking of this strange time of 'illness' he used to say that he had been 'away from himself' and unaware of the passage of time 'until that old lady came and prayed with me and suddenly I came to myself again.'

Some time later, when the Girls' School had been taken over by Mabel Jones, though I was there at Kigeme too, one particular girl did not return after the holidays. We received a message that she was ill 'with an illness the hospital doctors can't cure.' We immediately sensed that there were dark forces involved, and after enquiries we learned that her mother was involved in the rituals of the sorcerers. Mabel and I went out to the house, which was not very far away on the hills, and felt at once from the crowd gathered there that there were indeed satanic forces at work. We prayed in the Name of Jesus, claiming the protection of his precious Blood. The girl seemed unaware of our presence, and the people around asked us, 'Why have you come? Will she ever return to school?' We asserted that she would indeed be returning to school, and tried to address the girl. Words came from her mouth in a masculine voice, giving its name and saying that she belonged to 'them'. She then began, not in her own voice, to speak in words that sounded rather like a 'tongue'. I was disturbed, thinking, 'If a demon can make someone speak in an "unknown tongue", what have I been involved in?' At once there flashed into my mind with great clarity a phrase from one of Paul's letters (1 Corinthians

14:32): *'The spirits of the prophets are subject to the prophets.'* And I realised that I was indeed completely in control when I prayed 'in tongues', whereas this girl was in a trance. After prayer for her deliverance, we were able to take her back to school, where some of the other Christian students continued to uphold and strengthen her. One day while they were praying with her she seemed to go into a trance again, and a voice said, 'We don't want to let her go, but we cannot possess her heart because of that white bird that dwells there.' As the girl had made a Christian commitment we understood this to be a reference to the Holy Spirit (Dove) that indwelt her, 'white' being the word used for 'holy' in Kinyarwanda. After she had been cut off from these demonic influences through prayer, she was completely freed and was able to continue her education. Sadly though, her mother died soon afterwards while under the influence of witchcraft.

Meanwhile, significant changes were taking place in the organisation and leadership of the Anglican Church in Rwanda and Burundi as congregations grew and multiplied. From the earliest days the Anglican churches in the two countries had been part of the Diocese of Uganda. Then in 1951 Jim Brazier was appointed Assistant Bishop of Uganda with special responsibility for Rwanda, Burundi and Kigezi (S.W. Uganda, where the work of the Ruanda Mission had begun.) With movements for Independence in the early '60s it was felt that the time had come to make Rwanda-Burundi a diocese in its own right. Other dioceses were formed in Uganda and the Province of Uganda was created, of which Rwanda and Burundi were a part, the first Archbishop being Leslie Brown. In 1960 the then Archbishop of Canterbury, Dr. Geoffrey Fisher, came to inaugurate the new diocese, with celebrations at Buye in Burundi, whose church became the Cathedral. Then as national independence became a reality and the two countries developed their own identities, it became important for the diocese to divide into two and to have their own bishops. Bishop Lawrence Barham replaced Bishop Jim Brazier on his retirement and oversaw the separation of the administrative structures. A nominations committee, of which I was a member, was set up by the Diocesan Council to select three names in each country which were then sent to the Council of Bishops of the Province of Uganda for the selection of one name for each country. At Kigeme, on 6th June 1965, Adoniya Sebununguri was consecrated Assistant Bishop for Rwanda, and on 7th June, at Buye, Yohana Nkunzumwami was consecrated Assistant Bishop for Burundi.

I felt it a great privilege to be asked to prepare the Kigeme church building for the consecration. Kigeme was chosen because the building was at that time the largest church in the country and the newest - in fact, we were still in the process of completing it! I was asked to design and supervise the construction of a pulpit and lectern - and soon realised I had never studied these things closely before. How large should they be? how high? and where should the steps go up? However, with the help of local craftsmen we eventually managed to construct both, using bricks and breeze-blocks which looked in keeping with the rest of the building and seemed adequate and functional, especially after I had made a paper pattern for the top of the pulpit and lectern, so that the local carpenters could make polished wooden boards to cover the roughness of the bricks. I felt a special sense of relief when, at the consecration, Bishop Erika Sabiti (soon to replace Archbishop Leslie Brown as the first African Archbishop of Uganda) mounted the pulpit, together with Canon Ian Leakey acting as interpreter, and there was room for them both! Later I often preached from that pulpit myself, and had the joy of doing so again in 1988 on a fact-finding journey for a book on the history of the Anglican Church in Rwanda, and also in 1996 when on an international mission - and on both occasions found it as solid and pleasing-looking as ever!

Preaching from the pulpit in Kigeme Cathedral

In 1980 - fifty years after the Ruanda Mission was granted 'personnalité civile' - a French-speaking Anglican province was formed to include the dioceses of Rwanda, Burundi and Boga-Zaire, with an Archbishop chosen from each of the dioceses in turn. As the work grew, more dioceses were formed in each country.

During his first year in office, Bishop Adoniya visited the whole diocese and it was while he was at Kigeme that I shared with him my growing interest in Theological Education by Extension, whereby tutors visit students where they live, and supervise the work they do in their own homes, rather than students having to leave their homes and work to attend college elsewhere. I told him I would be interested in developing this method of training in Rwanda. Rather brushing this aside, he said, 'I have another idea.... While I was in England recently, I was taken to a wonderful place called Mary Sumner House (the Headquarters of the Mothers' Union), where they asked me if we had a Mothers' Union worker in our diocese. "No," I replied, "I didn't know such a thing was possible." "Well," they told me, "if you can find a suitable person we will pay her salary and provide a car". Now, Doreen, you know our language and our country - so, if you want to go round teaching the Bible in the villages, please will you be our Mothers' Union worker?'

To say I was nonplussed would be an understatement! How could I possibly fill such a role? - a single woman with no first-hand experience of the Mothers' Union, though I knew that several of my missionary colleagues (Julia Barham, Beryl Sisley and others) had introduced the concept of MU to the Christian women since early days, and used the MU ideals and prayers, etc, but no official recognition from MU headquarters had ever been sought. Further doubts arose from my perception of the MU at that time (quite erroneous as I was later to discover!) that it was a rather exclusive, jam-making, knitting, 'county' type of group. Added to all these doubts was the fact that I had long had a concern to teach the Scriptures more widely and academically, which had fired my wish to study for the London Diploma in Theology. In fact I had already made plans to sit the examination during my approaching home leave.

However, being firmly committed to the discipline of submitting to the leadership of the local bishop, I consulted my senior colleagues and the Home office of the Ruanda Mission, all of whom considered it could be a right move. One which, incidentally, would save them a missionary's salary, since I would be seconded to the Mothers' Union! The bishop's wife and others in the diocese were enthusiastic, not least because it would mean another vehicle being available for diocesan use! As it turned out, the MU headquarters were very happy for me to study for the London Diploma as well as attending their course for Overseas Workers at Mary Sumner House. So I had a sense that I was being directed in spite of my own reservations, and that it would be a good way of achieving my next academic objective. Accordingly in July 1966 I left for England and my further training programme in readiness for a whole new sphere of service in Rwanda.

Chapter 8

Widening Horizons

Greece, Holland, Colorado Springs, Cape Cod, Germany, studies, retreats, conferences - all combined to make the year I spent away from Rwanda as memorable and spiritually significant as any so far.

Shortly before leaving Rwanda in the summer of 1966 I received a letter from Harriet Corbin, the friend in the USA whom Corrie ten Boom had mentioned, inviting me most warmly to Colorado Springs for a holiday and time of fellowship with her and her husband. As the MU training course was not due to begin until later in the autumn I accepted most gratefully. Also, as it was possible to break the flight home from Rwanda to England, I stopped over for a few days in Athens, staying in the YMCA hostel and making day trips to many sites mentioned in the New Testament and in Ancient History - the Acropolis, the Colosseum, Corinth, Delphi and others. Next I flew to Schiphol to link up with Dutch friends of Corrie's, including Brother Andrew ('God's Smuggler'), well-known for his courageous and often dangerous visits to Communist countries at that time, taking Bibles for the Christians so eager for them. He told me about the Fellowship 'Open Doors' with which he had close links in England, and mentioned Noel Doubleday who ran a book distribution organisation, especially concentrating on books teaching more about Renewal in the churches around the world.

After I arrived in England, my former Domestic Science teacher, Miss Wakefield, knowing I now had no home base, offered me the use of a first-floor flat in her house in Reigate, which enabled me to keep in touch with my supporting church, St. Mary's, and join up with my many friends there. It was also near Reigate station, which made my journeys to London for MU and Ruanda Mission business relatively easy. My first concern, however, was to finalise arrangements for my America trip. It was so different being back where one could pick up a phone and dial Colorado Springs to chat over details of flights, etc. Corrie had also given me the names of two other friends of hers, Kay Anderson and Judy Sorensen, who ran retreats in one of their homes on Cape Cod for people seeking God's leading in a deeper walk with him. (Their two families had moved into the house of one of them, leaving the other house free for conferences and small retreats.) One of these retreats was, conveniently, planned for the end of my time in Colorado Springs. Somehow all the necessary bookings were made, a USA visa obtained, and I found myself on a plane heading for Washington DC where I changed for Denver. My hosts recognised me immediately at the check-out (I think I looked very un-American!) and carried me off along the freeway to Colorado Springs.

What an amazing time I had, with trips up into the Rockies for lunch, and down towards the Mexico plains for a taste of the desert, but most of all the opportunity to meet with many American Christians and share fellowship with them. The warmth of welcome and hospitality shown to me everywhere made me realise how we British must seem sometimes to be lacking in this compared with people from other countries. There was a delightful frankness too! On my second morning Harriet said, 'Today we go to the beauty shop!' [American for 'hairdressers!'] First though, she said I needed help with make-up - something I had long disapproved of! So I was shown the art of putting on lipstick and rouge, discreetly but effectively. Then we set off for the town. First the hairdresser made me relax for ten minutes. 'You are so tense,' he said. (Actually I was scared stiff!) Then came the shampooing, the styling, the setting. Next Harriet took me off to the dress store, and bought me what she considered to be a more suitable outfit than the clothes I had taken with me. The effect pleased her and she felt, I suspect, that now she could take me out and about without feeling embarrassed by my frumpish appearance! I wanted to go off shopping on my own another day, but she said people would not understand my English accent. I did manage a visit to the Post Office, which was quite a strange sensation - so unlike our Post Offices, and although everything was in English I did feel 'a foreigner in a strange land.'

My great hope for this American tour was to receive biblical teaching on the whole work of the Holy Spirit. Harriet had many tapes on the subject and I listened for several hours during my stay to various Bible teachers who were becoming known as leaders in the Charismatic Movement. On Sundays we went to the local Episcopalian Church, where I was impressed by their system of teaching. Everyone attended 'Sunday School', not just the children but all the adults as well, who were divided into different groups for the teaching/ sermon period, according to their stage of Christian growth and understanding.

During the week we drove into Denver, to an Episcopalian Church where there was a ministry of healing. I experienced for the first time the practice of the laying on of hands for healing as part of the Eucharist as we knelt at the Communion rail. After the service we all shared a meal, and again I was almost overwhelmed by the welcome and acceptance I received from everyone.

One of the experiences that stands out in my memory was meeting a German friend of Harriet's in her house. He had emigrated from Germany after the War, having previously been a Nazi, in fact an SS guard, before becoming a committed Christian. To pray with him was a very moving experience, as we remembered how we had been enemies during the War but now, in Christ, we were at peace.

Moving on to Cape Cod, I had further experience of the warmth and genuineness of American hospitality. Kay Anderson and Judy Sorensen met me off the plane in Boston, and as we drove to their home I could feel the differences there were between different States. In Colorado Springs I had felt rather 'foreign', but New England really did feel and look more like home. We stayed at Judy's house, Rock Harbour Manor, where a group of women from the Diocese of Massachusetts were gathered for a time of fellowship and retreat. Gradually I became more used to their freedom in prayer and worship, and their use of the gifts of the Spirit for mutual encouragement and building up in the Faith. For the first time I heard what I now recognise as 'prophecy', which was given especially when prayer for a specific situation or guidance about future planning was sought. These words of prophecy were always checked by the group, as were 'words of knowledge' and the 'interpretation of tongues.' One day Kay and Judy said they felt they had received a 'word' from the Lord which was for me as well as for them:

'I have set you apart for this work. Get your mind off the fruit: it is *My* responsibility, I am the Producer. These people are My responsibility. It is not even your responsibility to determine if you have been "in the Spirit" for even your mistakes are My responsibility. I AM God and able to do all things well - even to rectify your mistakes and show forth My glory in every one of them. Do you think I am a God who depends on the perfection of man to do My work? Is it My perfection and Myself that is to be shown and glorified. I have not set you forth to glorify your walk in Me, but My Spirit *in* you. These people are vessels of clay as you are, and do you think that I expect perfection - perfect wisdom operating in you at all times? No, I am but producing My wisdom in you and I will see to it that I reveal My glory. This is for your own sake that I tell you this - that you be not anxious about your every word and its effect, but that you learn to *rest* in My perfection and leave the responsibility for My Kingdom on My shoulders. I am *able!*'

Through the years that have followed I have often been encouraged and strengthened by the thought of the absolute sovereignty of God, even over my mistakes! And of the ultimate responsibility being on His shoulders.

For a while I was puzzled by another 'word' of prophecy that Kay and Judy felt was for me: 'In Europe will your future ministry be.' When I was later called back to the UK from Rwanda, however, I realised that this 'word' was given to Americans, for whom the UK *is* Europe!

Back in England, the rest of the autumn was spent in familiarising myself with the Mothers' Union work at home and around the world, and in completing their course for Overseas Workers. I was greatly impressed with what I found out about the MU at Mary Sumner House, at their alertness to the relevant issues of the day, such as the content of children's TV programmes, and standards of morality in society, as well as their excellent support for their workers around the world, providing them, as they put it, with 'the tools for the job' - transport, office equipment and other resources both material and financial for the running of training courses and other purposes. Spiritual support was given too in the 'Wave of Prayer'. Each day MU members across the world pray for a different diocese, which, because of the time system, means that prayer is continuing around the world all the time. Realising this used to thrill the African MU members very much.

I also followed up the suggestion Brother Andrew had given me in Holland that I link up with the Fountain Trust, an organisation founded by the Rev. (now Fr.) Michael Harper and others, to encourage openness to God through the renewing power of the Holy Spirit, which was being experienced across all the denominations in the late '60s. For perhaps the first time in 2,000 years of Church history we saw the Wind of the Spirit 'blowing where it listeth' - across all denominational barriers, as Christians met together for worship, recognising their ecclesiastical and doctrinal differences (les petites différences?) while increasing in mutual understanding and gaining rich insights from our different traditions, enjoying spiritual fellowship in the 'unity of the Spirit' as St. Paul writes in Ephesians 4:3. I found to my joy that several of my friends from school and later days were also being led into a fresh 'renewing' through this organisation. We attended meetings and seminars where the biblical background of charismatic manifestations were given, and were able to share in the deeply refreshing times of worship, when the consciousness of

God's presence was very real, especially in moments of spontaneous silence.

With Hilary Doubleday at Darmstadt

After much prayer it had seemed right to enrol for and sit all the subjects required for the Diploma in Theology in May '67, rather than taking it in two parts with a year in between as was usually the procedure, and what I had originally envisaged. I was most fortunate in that Meg Foote, Principal of Mount Hermon Missionary Training College in Ealing, invited me to spend the Spring term at the college, as a member of staff, free to use the college library and consult with tutors and attend any relevant lectures with those of their own students who were also sitting the Dip.Th. examination. New Testament Greek needed a lot of time, as the classical Greek I had studied at school was now very rusty! Several most valuable hours were spent with Margaret Jones, one of the tutors (now ordained), in Richmond Park, discussing the underlying issues of various questions from past examination papers. It was very much due to her help that I found my name on the pass list for the entire diploma.

During the Easter break and before the actual examination days, I had a wonderfully refreshing visit, spiritually as well as physically, to Darmstadt in Germany. Noel Doubleday of 'Open Doors' with whom Brother Andrew had put me in touch, had invited me to join him and his wife and two other friends, travelling in his Volkswagen combie through Holland, where we joined in a Sunday conference in Amsterdam. Towards the end, the leader said that God was giving him a special 'word' for Noel and me, so he called us forward and laid hands on us both, saying that we would be anointed with a new authority as we went forth in the Lord's name. I remembered this prophetic word when, back in Rwanda, one of the deeply spiritual African women, Hélène Murekezi, said to me, 'You know, since you returned from Europe you preach and teach with a new authority.' I realised that I *did* sense a new freedom to speak out what I felt the Lord was giving me to say, whereas in earlier years I had been somewhat bound by what I felt the 'brethren', the Revival leaders, would or would not have approved of.

Next day we continued our journey south. As we drew up at the German frontier post a uniformed official approached us with a stiff military stride. A rush of anti-German feeling came over me, arising from all we had heard and seen through the Nazi years, though I thought these feelings had been overcome in the States when I'd prayed with the former SS guard. 'Why are we going to *Germany*?' I asked myself, as I remembered again the disruption the War had made to my student days, the friends I had lost through death or separation due to military service. Then, as the official drew near he pointed to the words that Noel had had painted in German on the side of the van - *'Jesus died for our sins.'* 'Is that for me too?' he asked. 'My life is in a terrible mess. Can you help me?' So Noel talked to him for a while and we left him with literature to read and the promise of prayer. What a lesson that was for me! God sees us all as we are, sinners in need of His grace. I told myself that categorising people because of race or ideology, thus distancing ourselves from them and adopting a superior attitude, just will not do!

Arriving at Canaan, the Mother House of the Evangelical Sisterhood of Mary at Darmstadt, we were met by all the sisters at the entrance porch with great warmth. 'Welcome to our first retreat for English friends!' they cried. *English friends!* - yet it had been *our* RAF that had caused the devastation of Darmstadt on the 11th September 1944... Once again, I could only repent of my own earlier reaction.

'In everything God works for good with those who love him.' (Romans 8:28). In actual fact, it was as a result of that air raid that the Darmstadt Sisterhood came into being! During the years 1936 to 1944, two friends, Dr. Klara Schlink and Fraulein Erika Madauss (later to be called Mother Basilea and Mother Martyria) developed a number of Bible

study classes for girls hungry to study God's word. Under the National-Socialist regime in Germany all Christian work, especially among young people, was prohibited so they met secretly as, being high school girls attending Christian instruction, they were liable to find doors to higher education closed to them. However, most of the girls when put to the test were prepared to accept the possibility of deprivation in order to remain in the Bible study circles. In spite of this, the two leaders felt that, although they were faithful members of the group and acknowledged Jesus as their Lord, they lacked one thing - true repentance. The text the two friends had been given at the inception of the study circles was Matthew 3:2: *'Repent for the Kingdom of Heaven is at hand!'* They felt this was to be the watchword of their Fellowship.

On the day following that terrible raid when the city was reduced to rubble and a tenth of the population lay buried, the two friends picked their way through the shattered streets, past the charred remains of countless bodies, in search of their girls. Astoundingly most of them had emerged alive with their parents and managed to escape out of the burning town; a few had been evacuated previously. Even so, the two felt this was the end of their Bible study groups. Contrary however to all their expectations, over the following few days and weeks, one girl after another found her way back to them, feeling compelled to return, not only to see if their leaders were still alive, but to share their experiences of that fearful night. The Spirit of God had visited each of them, convicting them of sins they had previously not thought of as such, and they came to confess, matters such as lies or deceit at school, failure of charity at home, resentments, bitterness and an unforgiving spirit. Indeed they had experienced the overwhelming holiness of God through the imminence of death. They could now weep over their sins and sing for joy at the forgiveness of Jesus, which most of them received for the first time as a personal experience in their lives. A fervent love for Jesus sprang to life in their hearts, and prayer changed from petition to adoration. In spite of many difficulties during the following two years, many continued to meet regularly, and some began to live in Klara's house, where the vision was given to them of a Sisterhood which would be a small kingdom of love, with the duty of prayer, worship, preaching the Gospel and, above all, glorifying God by a life of faith. Many were the difficulties, frustrations and amazing answers to prayer that led up to the foundation celebrations of the ecumenical Sisterhood of Mary, on the 30th March 1947. The name had been chosen to remind them of the way of faith and living surrender to the will of God which was followed by Mary, the Lord's mother, as the first disciple.

By the time of our visit the Community had grown greatly from the original seven members, and smaller 'cells' had begun in other lands. The story of those early years is told in Mother Basilea's book *God is Always Greater*, and it was our privilege to hear and see in action the outworking of some of the chapter headings in that book which encapsulate their whole philosophy: God is greater than the impossible; God is greater than our everyday needs (these they literally 'prayed in' each day); God is greater than the Town Council's decisions; God is greater than the large sums of money we need. However great their need, God was always greater than that need. This conviction had governed the whole of their lives and been the dominating force in the history of the Order.

Another great principle of their spiritual walk - repentance, followed by cleansing and praise to Jesus (highlighted in Mother Basilea's book *Repentance: the Joy-filled Life*) - was so much part of the East African Revival that I felt at once a deep unity with them. Each Friday they held a special time of repentance for what the Germans had done to the Jewish people, identifying with their country and repenting that they, as Christians, had not protested or even sought to really discover what was happening during the War. They even went to Poland to ask forgiveness of the Polish people for Germany's treatment of them.

My deepest lesson during my visit came from Mother Basilea herself, who one day shared her own experience of 'life in the Spirit' and of the exercise of spiritual gifts. Something she used to say has stayed with me: 'If God is offering me gifts, how dare I say I don't need them?' I prayed that I might be open to all God's resources for the work he gave me to do for his Kingdom in the world.

So much that we heard and saw at Canaan deepened and broadened my understanding of the wonder of God's Kingdom. First of all, Canaan itself - so called because the Sisters felt it was to be an illustration or a demonstration of the Kingdom of God and its principles, and the utter trustworthiness of God in fulfilling his promises. For example, they had been granted the land as a result of some astonishing answers to prayer, but found there was no natural source of water on their property, and they were told that drilling for water would be no use as the geological formation of the area gave no hope of there being any. However, they were given a vision of a fountain and lake and 'river Jordan', so they prayed - and drew from their 'Promise Box' the text, *'Ye shall draw water from the wells of salvation.'* They therefore felt it right to instigate a bore. The engineers soon struck a source much stronger than any for many miles around! They made a lake, and a river and fountain - and as I stood by this fountain, springing up high and refreshing me as its spray fell all around, I was inspired by the knowledge it had been truly God-given.

The Sisters had also erected memorials which they felt God had directed them to make for His glory and praise, depicting the wonderful acts of God in other times - such as the Moriah monument showing the sacrifice of Isaac by Abraham and God's provision of a sacrifice in his place, reminding them of God's love in giving his own Son. They had also erected 'Stations of the Cross' to remind them of the way to Calvary. I found it hard at first, with my Protestant background, to enter into the meditations they led for us at these 'stations', but slowly I opened my spirit and began to appreciate the deep lessons they taught. More difficult, for me and others in our group, were the crucifixes not just in the chapel, but in other rooms. Why did they have so many around? Was not the symbol of our faith an empty cross? As we shared in worship, prayer and praise together, we came to feel that we could make our disquiet known. One of the group asked Mother Basilea about it. 'Well,' she said, 'First of all, remember we are Lutherans, so crucifixes are part of our tradition. Then, though we know that our Lord is alive and present with us, we think we need constantly to be reminded of what it cost him to redeem us. When we see the figure of Christ on the Cross, it is a reminder to us of what he had to pay to secure our salvation.'

This explanation was for me another lesson in being less critical and judgmental of the spiritual status of those whose traditions and outward forms of worship differed from those to which I was accustomed and considered 'more biblical', and in trying first to understand what these symbols or practices might be saying in the context of their cultural background. I was beginning to catch a fuller vision of God's mercy and grace as I drew nearer to those of other traditions, finding I could be enriched by their insights.

Before we left Darmstadt a ceremony was held for those of us who felt called to a closer prayer link with the Sisters and to become Friends of Canaan. I joined in this, to the particular delight of Sister Eulalia, who had a special ministry of prayer for Africa. She also promised to pray for me during the forthcoming Dip.Th. examinations and, indeed, sent me a most helpful prayer card at the time. We kept in touch, not only while I was in Africa, but for many years after my final return to England, when I was sometimes able to join in fellowship with the Community that the Sisterhood established at Radlett in Hertfordshire.

Returning from Darmstadt, I settled down again to my final exam revision, though there were also opportunities to join in various meetings and conferences, some organised by the Fountain Trust, and strengthen my links with Michael and Jeanne Harper, the Doubledays and other leaders in the Charismatic Movement. As well as carrying out official deputation meetings on behalf of the Ruanda Mission, I was invited to share in the leadership of an Inter-Varsity Fellowship mission to Exeter University, with Canon David MacKinnes, whom I had got to know at lunch-time meetings at St. Helen's, Bishopsgate, and Edgar Trout, whom the Lord had used in ministry to me at an earlier conference. I learned so much from these two Spirit-led leaders of the need for spiritual discernment, particularly in counselling people who may have had contact with the occult, and also the need for awareness of the reality of spiritual warfare and the power of prayer in the Name of Jesus. Part-way through the mission, Edgar Trout discovered that a group of Satanists were organising prayer against us, and so we were able to bind the negative powers by the authority of the Name of Jesus. Personally I had the joy of helping a girl who seemed to be under a dark cloud of oppression and who, particularly in the mornings, felt almost unable to continue living. Through prayer and explaining how to use the Name of Jesus against the sense of darkness and to proclaim 'Jesus is Lord!' over all her circumstances each day on waking, she was helped to reach a place of peace. Later she wrote to tell me how her life had been transformed, and of how she had shared this 'way' with a friend who had similar trouble, 'and what you taught me worked for her too!' she added.

Eventually, with the Mothers' Union training and the Diploma in Theology behind me, I left again for Africa, spending some time with the MU workers in Uganda, where the MU Movement had, for many years, made a great contribution to the building up of the Christian community. Then, picking up my new MU diocesan car - a Peugeot 204 estate, with the MU emblem on the door - I drove down into Rwanda.

Chapter 9
Mothers' Union work

The journey from the Rwanda border to Shyogwe where I was to make my headquarters was a most encouraging one. The country appeared much more relaxed, with fewer armed barriers at road junctions, and in the administrative centres considerable evidence of Hutu and Tutsi working together for the building up of a peaceful co-existence. Though the leaders of the Republic were mostly Hutu, Tutsi who had remained in the country appeared to have accepted the situation, and the expertise of some of them in clerical and other roles was being drawn upon. I soon found also to my great joy that it was possible, as in pre-revolution days, to travel freely around the country on safari and hold large meetings in the open air, which people attended freely.

In order that our Mothers' Union in Rwanda be officially recognised by the London Headquarters, we needed to draw up a Constitution to submit for their approval. Our first objective, therefore, was to form a committee to consider this. Catherine Sebununguri, wife of the Bishop of Rwanda, became national President, and a group of other leading Christian women of both ethnic groups helped in the planning of our movement. Initially we called ourselves 'Umutwe w'Abafite Ingo' (literally, the Fellowship of those who have Households - i.e. 'homemakers'), the idea being not to exclude the men, who were beginning to say, 'What about us!' Because of the preaching of the Gospel a different understanding of marriage had developed, with many - both men and women - seeing it as a partnership within which real and equal fellowship and responsibility was possible. The Mothers' Union Headquarters accepted our title and concept of a mixed fellowship, and though women did play very much the major role in planning and leadership, quite a number of men, especially out in the hills where we held large rallies, enjoyed taking part.

Some years later, however, the Rwandan women decided to alter their title, making it more exclusively for mothers - 'Abateg Urugore' - those who wear the 'urugore', the bamboo headband signifying the wearer has born a child. I understood the desire of the women to have an organisation that was very obviously their own, for in spite of the fact that

Christianity had given African women a new dignity and status, the Church was still very male-dominated, as was to a considerable degree the State. Nevertheless, in view of the fact that in recent years the worldwide MU has moved towards the concept of including men in their fellowships since they have equal responsibility with women of maintaining Christian family values, I was sorry that Rwanda had not kept its avant-garde vision.

In my M.U. car

From all over the country came a widespread demand for MU branches, so I felt the wisest strategy was to concentrate on the training of leaders. Accordingly, I formed a small team of able women to share in this programme. We invited potential leaders from different localities to come to Shyogwe for short training courses, for which the MU in London willingly sent out funds to help with transport and other costs. We had valuable times of fellowship and teaching - on the history and aims of the Mothers' Union and on subjects such as health and hygiene, child development, particularly the understanding of teenagers in these rapidly changing days, food preparation and cake-making (a great favourite!). Sometimes we travelled to outlying areas to hold these courses, and I followed them up by sending out a monthly programme to all branch leaders. This included a Bible study and other teaching aid material, as well as suggestions for practical work, such as a recipe or pattern for children's knitted or other garment. People in England sent us parcels of oddments of wool, which we distributed as they became available.

The movement grew rapidly in Rwanda and in a very short time we had twenty branches and over 2,000 members, and this growth has continued down the years. The image of the MU was a very positive one, and the rule requiring members to have had a Christian marriage meant that, in general, it was the more educated women who were eligible for membership. Many were teachers or nurses who could give a definite and informed lead. Soon a type of 'uniform' was developed, which included a sash with the MU emblem embroidered on it. Some branches in England having links with Rwanda sent out banners, which soon became very popular for processions in church, etc, and helped to heighten the profile of the Mothers' Union.

The leadership adopted as a slogan 'We are Christ's Lanterns' - based on the chorus, *'Jesus bids us shine like a pure, clear light ....'* - bringing light into the dark places, they said, and seeing with His eyes, discerning what is wrong in heart and life, and the reason for it. A practical illustration was in the case of kwashiokor, a protein deficiency which gave children skin trouble and bloated limbs and stomach. The traditional African view was that it was caused by witchcraft. The MU members kept their eyes open to spot such cases, explaining the real cause of the illness - that the young child had not been properly weaned when the mother's milk had dried up owing to another pregnancy, but had been given a sweet potato to chew, which was pure carbohydrate. They would then ask, 'Will you allow us to show you how to prepare good food for the child?' Then they would take cooked kidney beans, skin them and mash them, together with some dried milk, and also mash a banana with dried milk powder. Babies would eat these soft pastes more easily than beans in their skins, and the protein they were getting very soon made a great improvement in their condition. Then the MU members were able to give more teaching about the light that Christ brings, and were listened to. This health teaching had, of course, already been given by our hospital nurses, but the MU members had a wider acceptance and were able to be alert to cases of malnutrition in remote areas.

As might be expected, there came an ever-increasing demand for literature, for new as well as more advanced readers. It was because of this that I began to involve myself in translation work, particularly in answer to the needs of the MU members. I worked out simple reading and writing patterns which could be used among the women, and began to translate pamphlets on evangelistic themes as well as on practical subjects. At this time too I became involved with the Rwanda Protestant Council Literature Centre (CELTAR) at Kigali, being appointed its 'legal representative' with the Government.

It was in this capacity that I was asked to take part in a Bible Society Translators' course at Makerere University in Uganda, with a view to assisting in a new translation of the Bible in Kinyarwanda. The translation we were currently using was well over ten years old, and it was considered wise to make a revision of a first translation in any language after ten years, as any mistranslations, or faulty interpretations, will have become obvious by that time. The other delegate from Rwanda was a Roman Catholic Abbé, himself a Rwandan, with whom I had a most stimulating two weeks as we attempted to put into practice the translation principles we were learning in a 'united' translation of some New Testament passages. It was particularly illuminating for me to talk over aspects of the faith with a Roman Catholic and discover that he did have a personal faith in Christ and was not just following ritual observances, as I had previously tended to feel was the case with many Rwandan RCs. By this time Protestants were beginning to have more contact with Catholics - a real breakthrough brought about by Pope John XXIII calling us 'separated brethren'. In earlier years relations had been very bad, for the Roman Catholics, believing Anglicans and Protestants generally were heretics, preached, and sometimes acted, against us; we, on our side, felt they were not leading people to Christ but just into the church structures. Pope John XXIII and Vatican II broke down barriers of mistrust and initiated moves towards working together. So here was I, with my staunchly Protestant heritage, working alongside this Roman Catholic Abbé! (Another instance of God saying to me, 'Don't put people into boxes and write them off!')

One day as we worked on our translation exercise, the Abbé spoke of his discontent with the word the Roman Catholics used for Holy Spirit - 'roho' (Swahili for 'soul'). 'This foreign word does not mean for me the blessed Holy Spirit whom I know and love, and who guides me,' he said. We both felt that the translation Protestants used - 'Umwuka Wera' (literally, 'white breath' or 'white spirit', the idea of holiness lying behind the Kinyarwanda word 'wera' meaning 'white') - was nearer the concept, but that both needed interpretation.

Back at Shyogwe, the Abbé came to spend Sunday with us and joined in the service - something that would have been unheard of a few

M.U. Leaders Training Course at Shyogwe

years previously - and I also visited him one day at his seminary. This was the beginning of several contacts that I and others had with the Roman Catholic leaders; particularly valuable for me was getting to know the Pope's representative for ecumenical relations in Rwanda, Père Nothombe, who wrote several very perceptive books on Rwandan culture and beliefs. This opening up of relationships with the Church of Rome increased as the Charismatic Movement began to touch them also, with much more fellowship and even joint prayer meetings. A further step forward was the adoption of a common version of the Lord's Prayer for use in all churches.

Several new Mission Partners were coming out to Rwanda at this time, as well as VSOs (Voluntary Service Overseas), and I was asked to take on responsibility for their language study and cultural orientation. Most of them came to spend some months at Shyogwe for concentrated learning, and I would take them round the country with me as I visited the various MU branches or other groups. I was able to share with them my understanding of local attitudes and culture, helping them to become accustomed to the Rwandan way of life, while they were able to try out phrases they had learnt and listen to talks and sermons - getting their 'ear in' as it were.

I was fortunate that at that time Margaret Gooday was at Shyogwe, as she had considerable experience in methods of language teaching. Together we worked out a new study course using audio cassettes on which our African colleagues recorded a phrase, left a space for the student to repeat it, then repeated it again himself. We began with simple everyday phrases, which the student didn't see written down at first, to avoid adopting an English pronunciation, that he or she could use with Africans they met during the day. Gradually a vocabulary was built up and grammatical concepts introduced. The method seemed to work well, and in fact one of the Belgian Presbyterian missionaries, Monsieur Overdulve, asked our permission to translate the explanatory parts from English into French for use with their new recruits. He consulted with Dr. Coupez and Monsieur Kamanzi for tonal values and spelling, and in 1978 published a complete book, *Apprendre la Langue Rwanda*, in which he graciously acknowledged the methodology to be ours. The book was used by French-speaking workers in Rwanda for many years.

One of the outstanding experiences of this term of service in Rwanda was the opportunity to join in a big convention at Maseno in Kenya, led by Africans and Europeans who were experiencing charismatic renewal. The warmth of fellowship there was almost tangible, the teaching biblical and Christ-centred, and so reminiscent of the great conventions held in previous decades by the Revival Fellowship. There was one difference, however, in that more emphasis was placed on God's intervention in the 'gifts of the Spirit', and intervention too in a physical way, particularly in healing. I can still see in my mind's eye the radiant face of a Kenyan schoolmaster who had been healed of blindness; I don't know the details of his affliction, but his joy was unforgettable as he sang and sang, 'Yes, God is good; Yes, God is good; Yes, He is good, He is good to me!' Before this, we had prayed in our Revival meetings for people to be healed, but we normally expected this to be by means of God's gift of medical science, and the skill and care of nurses and doctors. There was also a feeling, sometimes expressed, that concentration on physical healing could place too much emphasis on the body rather than the spirit (not realising how closely connected are the workings of body, mind and spirit). Ever since my last leave in England, I had suffered severe pain in my right Achilles tendon which I had strained badly playing tennis with a friend whom I just had to beat! The pain was really severe, especially in the mornings and after resting for a while. During one of the times of ministry for healing I felt prompted to go forward on behalf of a relative whom I felt needed deliverance from an oppression she seemed to be under as a result of some occult involvement. As I stood 'proxy' for her and was prayed for, I felt a great sense of peace and joy. Then walking back to my seat, I realised my tendon was no longer hurting, and it hasn't done so since!

During the summer of 1969 we had the joy of welcoming Festo (later Bishop) Kivengere and Yosiya Kinuka to Shyogwe. As travel between Uganda and Rwanda was now possible again they had made a tour of various church centres, holding conferences and conventions, and I had particularly wanted them to come and meet the women at Shyogwe. As always these two anointed leaders brought deep and challenging messages from the Scriptures, and we felt the convicting power of the Holy Spirit - but somehow people were strangely silent. Then after another teaching session from Ephesians 4 on growing to maturity in Christ, Everina, one of the MU leaders, leapt to her feet. I sensed a spiritual break-through and whispered to Festo, *'This is real!'* With great authority Everina (quoting from Ephesians 4:15) said, 'Speaking the truth in love - we are not!' And she opened her heart to speak of the superficiality and lack of true openness and love she felt had crept into relationships, often through fear of political incorrectness, of wanting peace at any price, of not being faithful and truly loving when failing to challenge attitudes and standards that were not according to the principles of God's Kingdom. Many others followed, repenting of spiritual coldness, asking forgiveness of each other, and singing with great power the chorus of praise and joy for the precious cleansing of the Blood of Christ - so much used throughout East Africa and beyond wherever the East African Revival spread:

Glory, glory, Halleluyah!
Glory, glory to the Lamb!
Oh, the cleansing Blood has reached me,
Glory, glory to the Lamb!

Looking round on these radiant faces, most of them women in this particular meeting, I remembered again the vital role that the women and girls had played in the early days of Revival. They had been open to God's call to go out and share the liberating power of the Gospel which they themselves had experienced, not just locally but often at quite distant church centres. In meetings and services they would stand up and share deep insights from the Word of God, or from *Pilgrim's Progress* (for years the only other Christian book available in the vernacular). They spoke with a God-given authority, and earned respect as teachers, nurses and, indeed, wives and mothers, holding others to their own high standards - as also did many laymen, and also children. But this had changed over the years.

Although several influences may have contributed to this, the main one, I felt, was the too rapid rise of clericalism, especially in a country having a high view of authority. Theological training and informed leadership were, of course, very important, but the status symbol which the clerical collar quickly became, and the subsequent restriction of preaching and teaching to those having episcopal recognition, rapidly stifled lay initiative and enthusiasm, stemming that spontaneity in sharing Spirit-given insights which had been so important in the spreading of the Gospel. To quite a significant degree, I think, the Mothers' Union, with its officially recognised leadership, restored this role to the Christian women, and though their influence was firstly among their own members, it did also affect the community at large, for they gained their own role in the church structures - not only that of 'making the tea' (i.e. providing meals at conferences, etc. - which they do exceedingly well!), but also providing a means whereby able members would be noticed when candidates for offices in the church were being considered.

The morning after the last of our convention meetings, we gathered to wave off Festo and Yosiya on their journey back to Uganda. I returned to my office to collect up the necessary papers for a visit I was making to Kigali on official business and for supplies, little suspecting the complete change of direction my life was about to take. Just as I was leaving someone came up from the local trading centre with the mail, so I paused to glance through it. There was a letter from Meg Foote, the Principal of Mount Hermon Missionary Training College, where I had spent those weeks preparing for the Dip.Th. exams, so I felt I must read it although time was getting on. She described an exciting new venture for a mixed training college to prepare students for the 'cross-cultural communication of the Gospel.' The new college was to be inter-denominational and international, accommodating students from a variety of ethnic and cultural backgrounds, and would begin as a merger of three existing colleges: Mount Hermon (for women), Ridgelands Bible College in Bexley (also a women's college), and All Nations Missionary Training College (for men). It would be sited at Easneye where the men's college already was, just outside Ware in Hertfordshire, and it was hoped that it could begin in the autumn of 1970, under the name of All Nations Christian College. David Morris, the Principal of the existing All Nations, was to be Principal of the new college, and Meg Foote Vice-Principal. They had been praying about the composition of the lecturing staff and, recognising the need for a woman educationalist with a theological qualification and overseas experience, had been seeking the Lord's guidance - when Meg received a letter from me! As I fitted the requirements, would I accept a place on the staff?

My immediate reaction was, 'Oh no, not now! Not now we've just got going again after all the political upheavals and can travel around the country again sharing the Gospel. And what about the Mothers' Union work which has now really got off the ground?' Then my next thought was, 'Meg and the others are people who really listen to the Spirit, so I mustn't refuse their invitation outright, without sharing it with the brethren. Oh, if only Festo was still here! Why couldn't the letter have come before he and Yosiya left, so I could have asked their advice? Dear Lord, please guide me!'

The journey to Kigali was becoming urgent, so I set off. About halfway there I saw a car parked by the roadside. Festo's! They had stopped off to call on a friend, so they hadn't crossed the border into Uganda as I had imagined, but were waiting there having a break! I told them about my letter, and at once Festo said, 'Doreen, obviously I haven't had time to pray about this, but I do feel this is from the Lord.'

'But,' I queried, 'what will you Africans think if I go off and desert the ministry I've been given here?'

'I don't believe,' he replied, 'that we're necessarily meant to spend the whole of our lives in one small corner.'

Our ways parted; he took the road to Uganda, I continued to Kigali. As I met with one and another of my missionary colleagues in the next few days, I was surprised that there seemed to be a general feeling that this could be the right move. In particular Albert (later Canon) Brown, who was then our Mission Representative in Rwanda, said, 'Doreen, I'm envious! If I were offered such a post I wouldn't hesitate!' Then I shared the suggestion with Bishop Adoniya, who had asked me to lead the MU work in the first place, expecting him to thoroughly disapprove. But after pausing a moment he replied, 'We've had wonderful fellowship through the years, and it won't stop if you go thousands of miles away, but, yes, you go and train other young people to come out and work with us.'

Could this be the Lord's redirection? Suddenly I remembered the word of prophecy given to me in the States, that my future ministry would be in 'Europe'. Accordingly, I wrote to the Mothers' Union Headquarters informing them of the invitation. They replied very positively, saying they would regard it as an honour to have one of their workers at the heart of missionary training. Likewise the Ruanda Mission CMS considered it would be a most useful contribution that Rwanda could make towards the training of missionary candidates, and they would feel confident to send their recruits to such a biblically-based college, especially when my knowledge of the Rwanda-Burundi culture would help their orientation.

My farewell presentation as M.U. Worker

So within a very short time I was on my way home! Mabel Jones was appointed as my successor in the MU work, and my other responsibilities seemed easily transferred. But I felt my heart was strangely numb, as Rwanda seemed 'home' to me and I had built up so many friendships. As I sat in the plane at Kigali airport, waiting to leave Rwanda for good (as I thought), I felt as though I had made no decision myself but that it was something that was happening to me in spite of myself, and yet I could do no other. I wrote in the journal that I started for the journey, 'Lord, you know that I have only sought to be in your will throughout my Christian life. You called me so clearly to Rwanda-Burundi all those years ago; so even now I trust you to stop me in some way if this new move is not your will. Otherwise I go forward trusting that you will go before me.'

This prayer was not just for the new ministry in England, but for the journey ahead. It was November 1969 and I was not due to take up my appointment until March 1970, so I had planned a circuitous route home!

* * * * * * * * *

All Nations Christian College was indeed to be 'from all nations to all nations,' and I felt that my future usefulness would be increased if I gained some experience of other cultures and mission situations than just East Africa. So for my journey home I booked flights to India, Israel, Rome and Morocco.

Before leaving Africa, however, I had a few days' rest with some friends in Kenya. Staying with them at the time was a Palestinian Christian who headed a Pentecostal mission based in the USA. We had helpful times of prayer and fellowship, and he filled me in with useful information about the Christian situation in Palestine. During the course of one prayer session he was given a word of prophecy for me as I returned to Europe, ending with the words '.... and your ministry will extend to all nations.' I had not told him the name of the college where I was going to lecture, so I rather felt this mention of 'all nations' was another confirmation of the direction I had been nudged into taking.

Leaving Africa after almost twenty-three years of ministry, I flew from Nairobi to Bombay where I stayed in a guesthouse with other CMS missionaries. The drive from the airport had taken me through some of the worst living conditions I had ever seen - far worse than any I had experienced in Africa. People were living in shacks made of cardboard boxes, others were lying on pavements with no shelter. Dogs were prowling around, all skin and bone, and everywhere was an air of hopelessness. On the other hand, walking through the streets of another area I was amazed by the welcome offered me by the people I passed. One group who were celebrating a wedding warmly invited me to join the festivities!

My first visit proper was to Manmad in Maharashtra, where Joan Newton whom I had known in the Christian Union at Bristol years before was headmistress of an important secondary school for girls. She was a member of the Bible and Medical Missionary Fellowship (now Interserve), and she gave me opportunities to talk with her Indian staff and lead Bible studies with some of the girls. It was particularly moving to talk with a group she affectionately called 'the Tibs': they were refugees from Tibet who had fled with the Dalai Lama; he had personally asked if she could take some of these girls into her care. I remembered how, while at college, we prayed so much for Tibet and other lands closed to the Gospel, and marvelled that now, tragic though the Tibetan situation was, and still is, some who might never have heard of the Lord Jesus and his saving power had been given an opportunity to do so.

From Manmad I travelled to Aurangabad to join Gladys Shaw, with whom I had shared some of my missionary training, and who was now quite a well-known CMS missionary because of the very readable books she had written on her work in village India. Now I had an opportunity to share in this experience first-hand, though she also introduced me to some of the very scholarly lecturers and doctors in the local community, took me to temples and shrines, and taught me much about Hinduism and Jainism. The visits with her to some of the villages were an unforgettable experience, however, for we slept by the roadside on the wide grass verges, she in her jeep and I under the stars on a camp bed (she thought the jeep would be too cramped for me!). The oxen and camels came munching around, but Gladys assured me it was all right - and so it proved! I was surprised at the freedom there was to share the Gospel openly and of the relaxed way people listened and watched the magic lantern slides (much more primitive than we had in Africa) and talked openly. The local people fed us and on the whole I felt at home in the villages of India, which were not so different from African ones, though I had to get used to the removing of my shoes on entering a house. Our normal mode of transport was Gladys's jeep, but sometimes it was by bullock cart, which was another experience I won't forget! More strange were the temples, with idols smeared with blood and the street processions with idols being carried to different locations. I often had a sense of spiritual oppression in these places, an awareness, as St. Paul indicates in 1 Corinthians 10, that behind the idol there was a demonic spirit.

Next stop was Delhi, where a schoolfriend from Reigate days met me. Eileen Buss and I had shared many Christian experiences since Crusader days, and particularly a clear call to missionary service. She had been led to work in India with BCMS (now Crosslinks) after some years in the Civil Service followed by nursing training. One of the initiatives of hers in North India was the development of special courses for slow-learning children, and I was able to see something of the outworking of this project as we travelled around. From Delhi we visited the Taj Mahal (where I had my photograph taken sitting alone in front of it!) and saw many other ancient shrines and monuments of India's long history. Then in the villages I saw something of the literacy work among the women and girls, and met a number of the leaders in the Church. It was a helpful experience to be in a country where Christians were in the minority and where they did not, on the whole, come from the better educated or leaders in society generally - the reverse of the case in Africa. It seemed to me that the Church in North India was marked by this sense of being an often despised minority, and appeared somewhat weary and certainly lacking the exuberant enthusiasm of African Christians.

Frequently we travelled by train - another experience never to be forgotten! At the stations, where platforms would be crowded with people sleeping and beggars were ever hopeful of 'backsheesh', Eileen would stride through them all, leaving me to follow as best I could. Making her way into what seemed an already overfull compartment, she always managed to find us a seat! When the train arrived at a station, vendors would run alongside the train selling tea and curry puffs, etc. Everyone was friendly and helpful, and even when I travelled alone on one particular journey I felt quite safe. People chatted freely, asking my age and about my family, but in a courteous manner, and they seemed to feel a responsibility for my safety and comfort. One day we took a river trip on the Ganges near Benares (Varanasi), passing the Burning Ghats where corpses are brought for cremation. Another day we went to a Buddhist place of pilgrimage, where Buddha had preached his first sermon. I was distressed to see people going round and round this building, measuring their length on the ground in the dust and the heat, to gain merit as they supposed. While we were going round in a small group I noticed one Indian man particularly because of the excellent English he spoke, though I was surprised that he was dressed rather shabbily in an old raincoat, sandals and with a red scarf round his head. As we travelled back to town in the bus we found ourselves in the rear part, where the seats faced each other. This particular man was sitting opposite me. He began talking, and asked me where I came from. 'Rwanda,' I said, and was about to explain where it was when he replied, 'Oh yes, you had a revolution there in 1959 and a Republic was established.' He then went on to speak about the Rwandan economic situation and the present state of the country.

'How do you know about Rwanda?' I asked. 'Most people, even in England, have never even heard of it.'

He told me that he was Professor of Political Economy at the University of Kerala! We went on to talk about my role in Rwanda, and I told him something of the working of the Holy Spirit and the growth of the Church. I can never forget his comment: 'If Christians had really lived out the teachings of Jesus Christ, we would have believed long ago.'

He went on to invite me to visit him in Kerala, and I believe he sincerely meant it. How many university professors in England, I wondered, would dress like the poorest people, travel around on buses and welcome strangers in that way? As we left the bus the whole group with whom we had been sitting thanked me most warmly for talking with them - something which was rather unusual for Westerners it seemed.

We were invited to spend Christmas with Archdeacon Bob and Mrs. (Dr.) Grace Harland in Allahabad. He had been curate at Holy Trinity Church, Redhill, were Eileen and I had worshipped as teenagers. Grace had been one of the seniors in the Girl Crusader class where we had both been given such a solid Christian foundation. Several other missionaries joined us for the day, and I was able to gain more insights into the problems and opportunities of Christian ministry and outreach in a land where other faiths predominated. Later, Eileen took me to Kachwa, one of the leading Christian medical centres in Uttar Pradesh, and I met some of the medical personnel who were later to link up with me on refresher courses at All Nations Christian College, so it was helpful to have an idea of the situation in which they worked. It was interesting to be able to visit some mosques, and sense the different spiritual atmosphere here from in the Hindu temples. The absence of idols, and the proclamation of the one God, the God of Abraham, made me feel freer in spirit - though this was not an area of fundamentalist Islam, being in predominantly Hindu India.

To my regret I did not manage to visit Nepal, that other land 'of hills and valleys' associated with my call to Rwanda so long ago, but I did have a magnificent view of the Himalayas as we flew from Delhi to Tehran and on to Tel Aviv.

Six days in Israel proved a very precious experience. I had a sense from the beginning that this was the Lord's land in a special way. I had booked a room at the St. George's Church guesthouse, and took a taxi from the airport direct to Jerusalem. When I greeted the taxi driver with 'Shalom' he was delighted, saying, 'You know "Shalom"?' and took special care of me, pointing out interesting landmarks on the journey. Indeed, I was impressed by the courteous treatment I received from all the Israeli officials and others I encountered. At the airport, for example, because I was travelling on to Morocco, a Muslim state, and the Six Day War of 1967 was still arousing anti-Jewish feeling in Muslim lands, I asked the passport official if he would refrain from stamping my passport.

'Certainly, madam,' he replied, and gave me a separate certificate of entry to hand in when I left the country.

This was the first time on my journey that I was alone in the sense that I had no friends with whom I could stay. But the Lord had 'gone before me', and on my arrival at St. George's guest house I met an Australian couple from Coorparoo, where he was vicar, and at once we felt a bond of fellowship. We travelled around together, visiting the different Holy Places, and shared a taxi driven by a Christian Arab, touring from Galilee to Jericho. Particularly in Galilee was there a strong sense of 'treading in Jesus' footsteps.' There was also, of course, a military presence everywhere, but our progress was not in any way hindered, and there did not appear to be the tension between the two communities that has arisen in later years. However, one day I returned alone to the Mount of Olives for a quiet meditation and climbing up to the Mount of the Ascension I noticed a couple of rather dubious looking men following me. Perhaps it was unwise to make such a trip alone, but after years of travelling on my own in complete safety in Rwanda, I had forgotten how different other countries could be. The men began to 'chat me up', but just as I was beginning to feel uneasy, three orthodox Jews in their flowing robes came along, asked if they were troubling me and sent them packing!

Some of my most outstanding memories are of the Garden Tomb; the traditional houses (very small huts really) in Nazareth that were probably not unlike that in which Jesus grew up; bathing (or floating!) in the Dead Sea; and a trip to Haifa that I made with the chaplain of St. George's who invited me to share with him in a service at the chaplaincy there and also drove me up to see Stella Carmel, a conference and prayer centre run by CMJ (Church's Ministry among Jewish People). The views of the Mediterranean were unforgettable!

In Rome, where I had a stop-over on my way to Morocco, I was again on my own, staying at a hotel booked by the airline. Of the whole journey this was the least pleasant experience as I began to feel quite ghastly and suspected I had a touch of dengue fever picked up in India. In the morning I managed to force myself to take a short tour of the city, briefly visiting Vatican Square on my way to the airport.

It was a special joy, therefore, to be met at Tangier by Patricia St. John, who was the author of several popular Christian books, particularly for children, beginning with her prize-winning *Treasures of the Snow*. She had stayed with me in Rwanda while doing research for her book

Breath of Life, a history of the Ruanda Mission which the Ruanda Council had commissioned her to write. I had been her chauffeur and interpreter for much of her journeyings, and we had developed a good friendship - hence her invitation to visit her in Morocco where she had worked as a nurse/evangelist for many years, based in Tangier where her brother Farnham was Medical Director of the Mission hospital. Meeting him again brought back grateful memories of the Lord's guiding through the years, for it was Farnham who had signed my IVMF card when I made my pledge to missionary service all those years ago!

Patricia was well-known and trusted by the women who attended the hospital clinics, some of whom came for small Bible study groups, and by others in the villages around. It was a moving experience to share the sense of apprehension of fellow Christians in a land where meeting together might bring persecution, or at least stones being thrown, as happened to us in one particular village by youths calling out, 'Christian dogs!' When I showed a group of women a photograph of African Christians walking along to church carrying Bibles quite openly in their hands, they marvelled that such freedom could be possible. I also met some young people who had come to faith through Christian radio programmes, followed up by correspondence courses, and realised what a wonderful means of teaching and nurture of the Christian faith these can be, especially in lands where other means of sharing the Gospel are difficult. I was sad too to hear from them the dilemma they were placed in, for if they openly declared they were Christians, obtaining or keeping employment would be extremely difficult. It brought home to me the sacrifices that many people have to make who become Christians in non-Christian lands.

Although it was January, we enjoyed lovely spring weather and drove along the Atlantic coast, spending a morning walking the alleyways of Casablanca and visiting some missionaries there, before driving up into the foothills of the Atlas mountains. Finally, I boarded my plane for Gibraltar, experiencing the somewhat nerve-racking descent on the runway there that seems like a nose-dive into the sea! Then, after a brief visit to the town and a glimpse of the famous baboons, I embarked for the final flight home and a new stage in my life.

Chapter 10
All Nations and beyond

Easneye, the estate on which All Nations Christian College was housed, had been the seat of the Buxton family, from whom the college had bought the house and some of the surrounding land. The Buxtons were a well-known Christian family who, with their cousins the Gurneys and the Barclays, made an important impact on 19th century England. At Easneye the house itself had been built by the son of Sir Thomas Fowell Buxton MP, who had succeeded William Wilberforce as leader of the anti-slavery group and who had been responsible for the passing of the anti-slavery legislation and other social reforms through Parliament. When the house was completed in the 1860s it was dedicated to God in a small ceremony at the wish of Lady Hannah Buxton, widow of Sir Thomas, who prayed that 'the house should be a fountain of blessing that would reach out to all nations.' A hundred years later that prayer was fulfilled in a way she could never have imagined! Daily prayers used to be said in the main hall where the family and servants would gather round the impressive fireplace with its carved inscription, 'Do it with thy might' (i.e. whatever your hand finds to do - from Ecclesiastes 9:10). We ourselves often met round this fireplace and were challenged by these words.

The Barclay family, bankers and brewers, also bought a nearby estate at Hoddesdon, called High Leigh, which is now a well-known Christian conference centre and which meant that Christian leaders attending conferences could come over to All Nations to visit and share times of fellowship with us.

Plans for the merger of the three colleges that were to form the new All Nations Christian College were somewhat delayed owing to the need to adapt the buildings at Easneye and to construct a new block - all of which took longer than had been envisaged. When my appointment began in March 1970, therefore, I joined the staff of Mount Hermon Missionary Training College at Ealing, travelling once a week to Ridgelands Bible College to lecture to students there on Church History. In February 1970 I had resigned as a CMS missionary, but not as a CMS member, and indeed my contacts with the Society have continued through many years. I was soon invited on to the Council of the Ruanda Mission CMS, as my vicar at Redhill, Hugh Evan-Hopkins, had been all those years ago when his interest in Ruanda had initiated my own application to work there. For several years I also served on their finance committee. CMS, the parent body, appointed me to the Candidates' Selection and Training Panel, on which I served for several years. When Simon Barrington-Ward (later Bishop of Coventry) became General Secretary of CMS he invited me on to the Standing Committee of the Society (its executive body), and for several years I was elected to the General Council of the Society (its governing body). In retirement I have been made a Vice-President of CMS. It has been a great privilege to be at the heart of this great Society for so many years; it has enlarged and informed my understanding of the world-wide ministry of the Church - which was especially valuable when at All Nations we were seeking to train those preparing to be involved in this.

The next academic year we finally moved into Easneye, and the new College was officially launched. My lecturing assignment included Church History, African Religions, Missionary Anthropology, with input into the Missionary Life seminars led by Martin Goldsmith, himself recently returned from service with OMF (Overseas Missionary Fellowship). I also shared some of the Biblical Exposition, and in the supervision of students on placements in local churches and further afield. Added to this, much of my time was taken up with my tutorial group, who came not only for advice about course work, but on pastoral and other concerns, particularly as they sought clear guidance about their future sphere of service. Often we would have times of prayer about these issues, and not infrequently the question of a life-partner would arise - a subject I myself had had many arguments with God about over the years! In a mixed college it was easy for a couple, or one of them, to feel that, because they were placed in the same 'maintenance team' the Lord was guiding them to form a deeper relationship; or for someone to feel they were being called to service with a particular Mission agency because a special friend of the opposite sex was being called to that Mission. Some of them asked me, sometimes in public lectures, about my own experience of so many years of celibacy. I was able to say, with honesty, that the Lord is no-one's debtor, and gives far more than he appears to have withheld. However, in private I did share with some students as it seemed right the times when I had been faced with a difficult choice, for example the time when a relationship developed which could have led to marriage, but I felt clearly that I was being called to overseas service while the young man concerned did not feel that he was called to service overseas. There were other times during the years when my returning overseas prevented enriching and potentially romantic involvements developing, and times when I looked back with 'if onlys' and thinking I would probably by now have had a family and not be so alone. At such times I have been helped to repent of 'If only....' and proclaim that the Sovereign Lord 'knows the way that I take' (Job 23:10), and to remind myself of the Psalmist's confident testimony (in Psalm 18:30 & 32) that the way of our God is perfect, and he makes our way perfect. To my surprise, as old age comes upon me, I find that the 'if onlys' and wishful dreams do not cease, but have to be committed each time to the One who is preparing me for 'my unknown future', as Corrie ten Boom used to say, here or in His eternal service.

Interestingly, at All Nations it was the men students who seemed freer to discuss these things with me - perhaps appreciating a female point of view? Several very wonderful matches were made between students at the college in the years I was there, sometimes across the cultural and national divides. Some, mostly women students, have remained single and lead a fulfilling Christian ministry, while others met God's intended partner in their area of service. I still remain in touch with a number of former students, and pray especially for those with whom close links have developed, in Indonesia, the Philippines, Israel, Kenya, Uganda, Senegal, the Congo, Surinam, Chile and, of course, Rwanda, from where it was a joy to welcome students before my time at All Nations came to a close.

Fellowship with Christians from so many different lands was a most encouraging and challenging experience. They all had thrilling stories to tell of God's leading, guiding and amazing provision for their needs. Some came from poor backgrounds and struggling churches, even some of the English students, yet they proved God's faithfulness in providing fees, support in the vacations, etc. One year we had some, by our standards, wealthy students from Japan who, hearing that some of the English students were in financial need, went to the bursar and paid enough to cover their needs. People were very supportive of one another, in prayer and in practical matters. One student, now a well-known preacher in Chile, wrote back after some time there, 'Things are so tough in some of these situations, and you find yourself without that upholding fellowship we had at ANCC - perhaps people should be helped sometimes to cope without it even there!'

The ecumenical nature of the college also meant that people came into contact with, and learned to work with, those from different religious traditions. Students who came from one denomination would often find themselves led to offer for work with another denomination. Some went from ANCC to train for the Anglican ministry. Many are now in positions of leadership and influence all over the world.

We also developed close relations with different churches and groups in the towns and villages around us, many of whom welcomed our students on placements, giving them experience in preaching, leading services, children's work and pastoral care. One such was Gilston-with-Eastwick, an incumbency near Harlow. The rector, John Tyndale-Biscoe (a direct descendant of William Tyndale), had earlier in life been chaplain to the then Bishop of Burma, George West (later assistant Bishop of Durham). John and Margaret (Margie) his wife had also been members of the Oxford Group (later called Moral Rearmament), and had more recently come into contact with the Charismatic Movement and exercised a ministry of healing. A meeting for prayer and ministry 'in the Spirit' had not long started in their rectory, springing from an encounter with a lady from a nearby village at the Festival of Light meeting in Trafalgar Square in 1971. Discovering they were near neighbours they arranged to meet for prayer, and one or two other local ministers joined in too, as well as one of our college students who had a contact with one of the ministers. She mentioned that one of her lecturers (me!) would be interested in joining the group. Two of the other tutors joined me later. John had been used by the Lord to put the Rev. Trevor Dearing, then a curate in Harlow, in touch with the healing ministry of a Pentecostal minister, Peter Scothern. Trevor's ministry began to be transformed, and when he moved to a living on a council estate in Hainault, a small and at first seemingly unresponsive congregation grew within three months from nine to ninety. He invited John and Margie to join him on Tuesday evenings in a ministry of healing, and often I would go with them. The meetings grew and overflowed into the church hall next door. We saw the healing, delivering work of God as people were healed of physical problems, the deaf beginning to hear, and sometimes those strangely oppressed with what seemed surely evil spirits were freed.

One day as I was standing in the crowd at the back of church, Trevor began to give what came to be called 'words of knowledge', saying that there were people there with heart trouble, arthritic joints and other sicknesses that the Lord wanted to heal. Many had gone forward for ministry when he suddenly said, 'Years ago you broke the big toe of your right foot and it never healed properly.' This was so specific, not like the heart problems of which there were likely to be a fair number in any large gathering. And I knew it was me! Many years before on one of my furloughs from Africa, I had spent some time with a friend in

Bournemouth. One day, being still very athletic, I started doing cartwheels and handstands on the sands. Over-confident, I lost my balance and came crashing down on my right foot. My toe was agony, and I limped around for weeks having a full deputation programme and no time to seek treatment. Some time later a medical colleague said I had obviously broken the joint, but that it had set after a fashion so there was nothing that could be done. Often it troubled me if I wore shoes with a high heel. At All Nations I had mentioned it to one of the students who was trained in orthopaedics, and he said I would have trouble with it as I grew older and eventually would be unable to put on a normal shoe.

So, in the meeting at Hainault I tried to push my way through the crowd, but the service ended before I could get near the front and those ministering healing. Nevertheless, I felt that God had spoken and perhaps I could claim healing in faith without further ministry. However, as it did hurt again from time to time I went to Harlow Hospital where the consultant said it might be possible to break the joint and reset it, but it would mean a long time in plaster and might not be improved. In any case there was a very long waiting list for non-urgent operations, and I never was called for the operation!

Several years later, when living in Nottingham, I heard that Trevor Dearing was coming to minister at a Pentecostal church in Aspley, near where I was living. My toe did still ache quite a lot so I decided to go along. I met him as we were both parking our cars in the car park. He was surprised to see me after so long. I explained the history of 'the Toe'. 'Well, we must pray for it tonight,' he said. At the time of ministry I duly went forward and he prayed with great authority for my freedom from pain and trouble with the toe, and I fell back 'in the Spirit' into the arms of one of the ministers standing behind. Since that day I have never had any pain in that toe, even when wearing shoes with high heels, and have full movement in it although the joint did not slip back into place - it remains as evidence of the injury, and the healing from pain and lack of movement that I received.

My fellowship with the Tyndale-Biscoes deepened as we met weekly for prayer, and experienced many answers to prayer among ourselves and friends for whom we were asked to pray. Then in 1972 John felt led to hold a 'Service of Power and Praise' in St. Botolph's, Eastwick, where the church was celebrating the centenary of its restoration. It held about 180 people; as the village was small we had expected perhaps forty, but the church began to fill up and we had to rush for more chairs. Trevor

Dearing, whom we had invited, brought a group with him from Hainault in a minibus. As it obviously met a need in the area, it was decided to hold these meetings monthly. I shared in the time of ministry, praying and laying hands on people for the Lord's touch at their point of need. Sometimes as I prayed the person would fall gently backwards and 'rest in the Spirit' for a while before returning to their seat. This phenomenon has been criticised in the belief that people are pushed over. I know that I did not push, and some people I hadn't even touched. We sometimes had most inspiring times when people who had come to the services shared their stories of how the Lord had healed them, physically, emotionally or spiritually.

At this period in the growth of the Renewal Movement many people were considering the question of Christian community living. Several communities were set up in various parts of the country. At Gilston Rectory John and Margie already had two former Moral Rearmament colleagues living with them, and one day at a 'Praise and Power' meeting they met three students from a nearby College of Education who said they felt called to some kind of community living. These girls moved into the Rectory, which was very large, and John and Margie asked if I would like to join them and share in the ministry of the home. Although I had a very pleasant flat in the old stable block at All Nations I felt it would be right to join them at Gilston while still retaining my flat as a base. It was certainly a most interesting, and at times difficult, year adjusting to community 'give and take' and trying to understand the wide differences of background, age and experience. We took turns with the catering - so diets varied greatly! - and basic chores. Sometimes we were able to give help and ministry to one another, and also to others from the locality who came to us in some kind of need. At the end of the year the students graduated and moved off to different occupations (one becoming a nun). I also moved out, while continuing my close fellowship with the Tyndale-Biscoes.

Life at the College continued to be stimulating and challenging. Each academic year brought more and more applicants, and the academic standard continued to rise as we had to be more selective. Students began to study for university degrees as well as the Diploma in Theology, and for some time now the College has had its own Postgraduate Department. Each fresh intake of students from many lands brought with them their own particular contributions to our life and worship. Short refresher courses were also held each year when missionaries and national workers from many different areas joined us. This was most enriching, and has meant that I still have friends in a wide variety of places and situations. Each year also we held a special course in Islamics, led by Martin Goldsmith, and to which I contributed. One year I took a group to the East London Mosque, arranged for us by the Rev. Canon Patrick Sookdeo. We were most graciously received by the officials at the mosque, who allowed us to be present at a time of prayer, and each of us was presented with a splendid copy of the Koran in the latest English translation with full explanatory notes. Likewise we invited Muslim speakers to All Nations to share their faith with us first-hand.

The estate at Easneye was large, and we were free to walk around as we wished. I was able to have an allotment which I thought would help to maintain adequate exercise and fresh air intake! I was soon growing my own beans and tomatoes and experimenting with other crops. I had not entirely lost my farming instincts!

* * * * * * *

After eight years on the staff at All Nations it seemed right that I should move on to a different sphere of service, since the Principal, Vice-Principal and I were all due to retire at the same time, and it was easier for me to be spared than they. After much prayer and putting out feelers in various directions, I was invited by CMS to be their Area Secretary for the Dioceses of Sheffield and Southwell. Although I knew Sheffield was 'somewhere up north', I had never heard of Southwell, in which Diocese CMS were now asking me to look for a house. My predecessor had lived in Sheffield, and it was felt that a change of residence for the Area Secretary would be a good strategy. Nottingham seemed as if it would be a suitable base, and Graham, my predecessor, indicated for me on a street map an area which he felt would be the most convenient for access to the surrounding area. I knew that Meg's brother, Dr. John Foote, was studying for ordination, having retired from his post as Pathologist at Nottingham University Hospital, and was selling his house in Nottingham prior to taking up an appointment at a church in Sheffield; when I asked whereabouts the house was I discovered it was opposite the Goose Fair site by the Forest Recreation Ground - almost at the spot Graham had indicated! Consequently CMS bought the house for me. Just behind the 'White House' (as it was called!) was the Clinical Theology Centre founded by Dr. Frank Lake (himself a former CMS missionary), to which people came from far and wide for courses and counselling. So I had a very distinguished neighbour!

As the house was large and my former school-friend Eileen Buss, whom I had visited in India, had just been appointed by Southwell Diocese to work with inner city churches and other groups in Nottingham, helping them reach out to their Asian neighbours, CMS agreed to her sharing the five-bedroomed house with me, which she did for three years before retiring to Folkestone. The contacts she made with local churches and with the Asian Christian Fellowship were helpful in providing me with openings where I might not have found them so soon.

In many ways I look back on those years as a CMS Area Secretary as among the most fulfilling and enjoyable of my whole ministry: travelling many miles each week, visiting CMS-supporting and other churches as invited, preaching and speaking about the World Church and how to deepen our partnership with them. I received in these two Dioceses an unexpectedly encouraging view of the Church of England, for in so many places I found groups of really committed people wanting to share their faith and increase their involvement with Christians in other lands. Of course, I recognise that the churches I visited were not necessarily typical of the Church as a whole, for it is largely only the churches with a vital life and outward vision that invite a missionary speaker!

The fellowship shared in the 'Northern Team' of Area Secretaries in the Northern Province of York was a happy experience. There were seven of us. Each month or so we met in each other's homes in turn, to pray and plan joint exercises and share fellowship. This meant that I travelled often to Newcastle, York, Bradford, Manchester, Chester and Lancaster. Every year we organised together a CMS Northern Congress, which was held at different venues across the North. A principal speaker and supporting team, often of overseas leaders, would come and lead groups and seminars, and visits to local places of interest would be included. Conference members would stay with CMS members in the area. In my last year as Area Secretary, the Northern Congress was held in Nottingham, and I was able to draw on the help of local CMS members to help with the planning. Our main speaker on that occasion was the then Archdeacon of Nottingham, the Ven. Roy Williamson (later Bishop of Bradford and then Southwark).

The Provost of Sheffield at that time, the Very Rev. Frank Curtis, had himself been an Area Secretary of CMS, so he was particularly understanding and helped me gain access to churches of widely differing churchmanship. He also invited me to preach in the Cathedral. I believe I was the first woman to do so! Another initiative of his was to invite the representatives of other missionary societies, so we could pray and plan together. The Bible Society Secretary, Rev. John Prothero, told me at the first meeting that he remembered me from one of my deputation meetings at St. Luke's, Watford, (on my first furlough!) when he was leader of the Youth group there, and his mother was the Ruanda Secretary for the parish! He lived in Nottingham so we often travelled up to meetings together, and friendship with him and his wife have continued down the years. I was grateful too to meet and get to know Edwin Ward, the Secretary for USPG (United Society for the Propagation of the Gospel). This helped to dispel another misconception I had long held, of USPG being 'High Church' and emphasising ritual rather than personal conversion and a biblical basis to daily living. Working together with Edwin and others in the Society made me realise how wrong such 'blanket' categorisations can be. Edwin had been working in the area for several years, and was well known in both Dioceses, and he most helpfully invited me to share with him in Diocesan and Deanery meetings which he arranged on a regular basis. On one such occasion one of the clergy said, 'You two work together like Morecambe and Wise! You must spend a lot of time preparing these times.' Actually we didn't. It was just that we had achieved an understanding of purpose and approach.

At one clergy chapter meeting in Southwell Diocese, at which we hoped to encourage missionary interest and involvement, I asked the group of clergy, 'Do you see it as part of your ministry to challenge your congregations about vocation? I don't mean necessarily to go overseas, though that might well be so, but to ask the question, "Is God calling you to stay where you are? If that is so - fine! Otherwise, where does He want you to be?" One of the clergymen, in whose house we were meeting, got up and went into the kitchen where his wife was preparing the coffee. Returning after a moment he said, 'I want to take up what Doreen said and challenge my congregations as she has suggested. But I also realise I mustn't do this without first being open to the challenge myself. I've checked with my wife, and want to say before you all that we're willing for God to direct us anywhere He will.' Three weeks later he rang me up. 'Doreen,' he said, 'you don't know what you've started! We believe God may be calling us to South America!' Accordingly, as his sabbatical was due, he visited several South American countries, and while in Uruguay was asked if he would consider becoming vicar of Montevideo. On returning to Southwell Diocese he shared this call with others, and it was felt to be right. So the family moved to Uruguay, and after a short time he was appointed Bishop! Then in 1998 he became Bishop of Peru.

Southwell Diocese has formed a close link with the church in Uruguay, as well as an interest in Peru, which will continue.

During my four years as Area Secretary most of my Sundays were of necessity spent in different churches across the two Dioceses, but I did begin to form closer links with one or two, especially St. Margaret's, Aspley, in Nottingham. This had come about through an All Nations link; when I told the students about my new appointment and that I would be living in Nottingham, one of them, a doctor from the Shetland Islands, mentioned that his sister was married to a curate in Nottingham, and said to get in touch with him. The curate's name was Martin Oram. I did make contact with him and attended his church, St. Margaret's, Aspley, as soon as I could. The vicar at that time was Rev. John Finney (later Bishop of Pontefract), who had initiated regular 'Praise and Power' services in his church, to which people came from across the Diocese, inviting well-known speakers in the Renewal Movement - David Watson, Michael Harper, Bishop Richard Hare, Trevor Dearing and others. They were moving and encouraging times and I tried to be there as often as possible. Actually, on my first visit John Finney himself was preaching; it was right at the beginning of my time as Area Secretary and I had been battling for some time over certain circumstances and events in my personal life that I found hard to understand. As I sat there a private argument with God was going on in my mind, and the thought that was uppermost was the one I so often battled with, 'It isn't fair!' At that precise moment John said in his sermon, 'You may well say, "It isn't fair," but the Bible never says it will be "fair". God is Sovereign, He is just, and allows and over-rules events for good as we leave ourselves in His hands.' I could hardly believe it, and felt truly chastened and repentant. At the time of ministry I went to ask for a special anointing for my new ministry with CMS, and again as he prayed John was given a word of knowledge that answered the thoughts that were in my mind but which I hadn't mentioned to him. Later I shared these experiences with him and his wife Sheila when they invited me to lunch at the vicarage, and a friendship began which has been a strength and inspiration since that time. I joined a house group that he led at St. Margaret's, and gradually became more involved in the life of the church. When he set up a Diocesan Renewal Fellowship he invited me to join, and here I met clergy and others from Southwell Diocese and nearby whom the Lord was leading forward into a ministry of healing and spiritual renewal.

By the time I was due to retire from CMS, John Finney had left St. Margaret's to become the Diocesan Adviser in Evangelism, and the Rev.

Ray Lockhart had come to the living. He felt it would be helpful for the church to have an Administrator as a member of the staff team, but funding was a problem. I realised that I had that kind of experience after all my years of administration in Rwanda, and that I could possibly manage on my pension, which was now due. They were, in fact, able to offer me a small honorarium; and so I became an Administrator and Reader at St. Margaret's, moving into a house on a council estate in the parish, where many were unemployed or were one-parent families. My next door neighbour was a miner, as were many on the estate, and when the miners' strike broke out he would not strike but joined the UDM as did many in Nottinghamshire. 'We've got our mortgages to pay,' he said. (Many council tenants were buying their own houses at that time.)

As so often seems to be the case in Anglican churches, most of those in leadership at St. Margaret's lived on the private, middle-class side of the big main road that ran through the parish. Not many people from the council estate attended the church. Some who came to the Mums' and Toddlers' group from that side said their neighbours didn't want to come to church because they were a 'toffee-nosed lot!' We thought and prayed about this, and one day I made the suggestion of having a Sunday morning meeting in the large day school right in the middle of the estate, as people were used to going there to take or fetch their children and to attend school functions. We felt it was worth a try, so I talked to the headmaster and the caretaker, who agreed to our using one of the larger rooms that had a kitchen unit so we could make drinks. Next a team of church members started visiting and inviting people to the meetings, which would take more of an inter-denominational form, as several of those contacted were not Anglicans. Soon quite a regular congregation built up, including some who had originally been attenders at St. Margaret's; and when there were special services for the whole parish, people from the estate were much more willing to cross the hitherto forbidding portals as they were among people they had come to know. As time went on, this venture became what is officially known as a 'church plant', with one of the St. Margaret's clergy assuming special responsibility for it.

Another initiative we took at that time was in response to the cry of the Christian young people at the church: 'There's nowhere we can take our friends in the evening except the pub!' This was an era of the blossoming of Christian Coffee Bars across the country, so we began to pray about the possibility of such a project. Some members of the church had already pioneered a charity shop called 'Green Pastures', selling second-hand clothes and books etc, and Traidcraft articles. Just at the time we were praying for a Coffee Shop, the shop next door to 'Green Pastures', which was on the main shopping thoroughfare, went up for sale, but before we could get organised it was bought by a retired furniture dealer. He made many alterations, rewired it and moved his furniture in. We were perplexed that such an ideal site should have been snapped up from under our noses. Then with what I believe was a word of faith, I said, 'He's getting it ready for us!' We continued to pray, and within a very short time the owner called in at 'Green Pastures' and asked if we wanted to buy the shop! He said he'd wanted something easy to do in retirement but found he was having to work as hard as ever, so was going to live in his bungalow at the coast. Quickly we contacted all those whom we knew were interested in the Coffee Shop project and visited nearby churches to share the vision with them. Next we held a coffee morning to give information about the Coffee Bars and their outreach; and we had a pledge box for people to say what they would be prepared to give or covenant. It was held on a dull wet Saturday morning and not many people seemed to come in, but when we opened the pledge box we found pledges for over £18,000 - more than half the price of the shop! Consequently we felt it right to go ahead in faith. We founded a Charitable Trust (having charitable status meant we could reclaim tax on covenants). I wrote to Boots the Chemists, who have a 'charity committee', explaining that a number of their employees lived in the parish and they would benefit from the shop. They responded with a gift, as did other groups we approached, and one of the church members who was a Bank Manager helped us obtain a loan for the rest of the money. So the shop was bought, redecorated and refurbished as a restaurant. I wrote to the local manager of the Pork Farms chain of shops (who later trained for the ministry and became commercial chaplain to the Nottingham stores and businesses) asking if they ever had spare cold display cabinets when they revamped their shops. He sent us a very nice one almost by return!

We decided to call the shop 'Light Refreshment' (with a deliberate double meaning of course) and had an appropriately challenging sign outside. At first we managed with a volunteer staff and a manageress, and served breakfast, lunches and teas. Another team was responsible for the Coffee Bar in the evenings, and local Youth groups used it in turn. We also had a member of the team available to talk to or, if need be, counsel and pray with anyone who was lonely or in need. The shop became very popular and before long we had paid off the loan and set up the upper floor as an office and meeting room. We were so pleased one day to have reported to us a conversation overheard at the nearby bus-stop.

'What's that shop "Light Refreshment"?'

'Oh, it's a sort of tea-shop, but you get another sort of refreshment as well!'

The shop certainly became a centre of Light and Refreshment for many in the neighbourhood.

* * * * * * *

One day I received a letter from Canon Leslie Morley, Rector of St. Peter's Church in Nottingham City Centre. We had first met in my early CMS Secretary days, when he was a Residentiary Canon at Southwell Minster, responsible for services and events in the Minster, and I was planning a CMS evening there for the whole Diocese. We had kept in touch from time to time, and now he wrote to say he had a vision for a week-day ministry at St. Peter's, where he had just been appointed, and wanted to build up a team of Pastoral Assistants to be in the church and ready to welcome visitors, talk with them and, if appropriate, offer prayer. Would I consider becoming a member of this team? I felt this was a new opportunity for a different form of outreach, and accepted initially for one day a week. At the same time I was beginning to feel that the administrative part of my work at St. Margaret's was becoming more and more demanding, and that it was time for the church to consider the appointment of a full-time paid Administrator. My other involvements were also demanding, for as well as my involvement with 'Light Refreshment' I was responsible for the drawing up of programmes for house-group studies and training prospective house-group leaders. On the wider scene I was Administrator of 'New Way Nottingham', a group formed in connection with the National Initiative in Evangelism and which consisted of ministers and leaders from different denominations in and around Nottingham. We held Ministers' Breakfasts once a month, and planned joint outreach events. It was the time when the idea of Christian Camping Conventions was beginning to spread. I remember floating the idea of holding such a week on the Newark Showground in Nottinghamshire, and finding myself with the responsibility of organising it! It was an event that ran fruitfully for some years.

Changes were in the air, for about the time I relinquished my role as Administrator at St. Margaret's, Ray and Jill Lockhart felt they were being called to Israel to work with CMJ and would be selling the house they owned on the Aspley estate where I had been living. I heard of a small Charity who had warden-aided bungalows and flats for 'widows and spinsters'. Applicants were supposed to have some Anglican or other church connection to provide the community with some uniting bond - in fact one of my friends, herself a Vice-President of CMS, already lived there. I was accepted and moved into a little bungalow, though I had to dispose of most of my family furniture, which local housing charities for the homeless were grateful for. The housing complex was on the other side of the city centre from Aspley, so gradually I began to withdraw from weekend activities at St. Margaret's as St. Peter's was so much easier to reach.

So began another of the 'recycling' periods that have characterised what people refer to as 'retirement'! My Reader's licence was transferred to St. Peter's, and I began taking my share of the activities in this inner city church - leading services, preaching, leading mid-week groups and, in particular, spending two or three days in the church welcoming visitors.

Owing to its position in the heart of the shopping centre many people dropped in - local people coming for a quiet break in the middle of a busy day, visitors from overseas, and needy folk who drifted about the inner city. There was a coffee room where light lunches were served, and many people would come in, some of them glad to have someone to talk to. Sometimes more dramatic things would happen, for example when a man came in having cut his wrists, though not very badly. We were able to talk with him while an ambulance was called. Others in material need and other distress would come in wanting financial help. We had a rule that we did not give money, but if there seemed to be a real need we would ring up Emmanuel House, a day centre run by a city centre Roman Catholic church, and tell them the name of the person we were sending round. At the end of the month we would repay Emmanuel House for the meals they had supplied. Many other visitors wrote prayer requests in a book we provided for the purpose, and these requests were remembered at the Communion services and by those of us on duty as we paused by the prayer desk when there were no visitors needing our attention.

One day a group of young people rushed in, raced around the aisles, and went up into the pulpit and choir stalls. (I learned later that they had all absconded from 'secure accommodation'.) One young boy of nine or ten went up to the candle that was burning in front of Rublev's 'Ikon of the Trinity' and blew it out. I strolled up to him and asked why he had wanted to blow out the candle. He made no reply but looked at me with a blank look in his eyes. I told him the candle was to remind us of Jesus, the Light of the world, who loved him and wanted to come into his heart.

The boy just continued to look at me blankly. By now the others had joined us and I guided them back into the porch. On the way one lad asked, 'Why do you wear black?' (I had my cassock on.) 'Are you a nun?'

'No,' I said, 'but it's a special type of dress we wear to show we're part of the work that goes on here, a bit like pop groups wearing leathers and gear that mark them out as group members.' 'Oh yeah, I see,' he replied.

'Don't you find it boring?' asked another. I explained a bit about the wonder of being where God is specially worshipped and getting to know Him more. As we moved into the porch a teenage girl said with real earnestness, 'Tell me more about God.' Words of personal testimony brought them all round listening. Then one boy took a handful of what looked like cigarette ends from his pocket and offered me some! 'Thank you so much,' I said, 'but I don't smoke.'

'Don't you smoke pot!' he exclaimed incredulously. Then, turning to the lad who had blown out the candle, he said, 'He's high on it' - which explained the blank look I had been puzzled by. Then they all thanked me for talking to them and left. The next day I heard that the boy who had blown out the candle had rushed out into the street and been killed by a bus. I prayed that in that last moment he would have remembered the words I had spoken about Jesus and His love for him.

Another lunch-time a couple from Pakistan came to look round. I asked if they were members of the Church of Pakistan. 'No,' they said, 'we're Muslims, but we love going into places where God is worshipped.' They had been travelling widely, and were going on to America when they left England. Looking round they asked, 'What is this? Church of England? What was it that made the split into Catholic and Protestant?' I decided it wasn't the place for a Church History lecture, and at the risk of being too simplistic took up a Bible from a nearby pew and pointed out how, in the 16th century, some people had realised as they began to study the Bible more closely, that some of the teachings and practices that had grown up in the official Church were not founded on the Bible's teaching, and that the Reformation was, in brief, a desire to get back to the Bible as the basis of belief and practice. 'That was right, wasn't it?' they responded!

The time for our mid-week Communion service was drawing near, and they asked me about it. I explained that we gathered together to share bread and wine as Christ had done with His disciples at the Last Supper, in remembrance that He died for our sins on the Cross.

'They never found His body, did they?' they commented.

'No,' I said, 'He rose again and is alive and with us here now.'

'Yes, we believe that,' they replied.

I gave them the service book to look through while I went to the vestry to tell the rector that he had a Muslim couple who were going to worship with us! He explained the service as he went through it, and the husband came up and received the bread, but not the wine, while his wife remained in her seat. After the service they thanked me and offered me sweets, saying, 'Please share these with us as we have shared with you.' I gave them a copy of St. Luke's Gospel that we were distributing at that time. 'Thank you very much,' they said, 'Please write in it and put your address. Here is ours and we would be so happy if you would visit us in Lahore.' I still remember them from time to time, and pray that the Gospel of Luke is being read.

St. Peter's had a small lending library, a shelf of well-chosen books of a devotional nature. It was here that I noticed one day a book entitled His Life is Mine, and the title drew me straight away. It was written by the Archimandrite Sophrony, a Greek Orthodox monk who had spent many years in the monastery of St. Panteleimon on Mount Athos, and had later founded a monastery at Tolleshunt Knights in Essex. This was to prove to be another of the landmarks in my spiritual pilgrimage, for it introduced me to the riches of Orthodox spirituality.

In 1945, while still at the CMS Training College, I had been sent for a weekend conference in Oxford of the Fellowship of St. Alban and St. Sergius, a Fellowship established for closer understanding between the Anglican and Orthodox Churches. In spite of my 'evangelical prickles' I had appreciated much of the worship and teaching. Now, forty years later, I was much more open to the way God spoke and led people of very different religious traditions from mine. This awareness of insights from other traditions had been increased by meeting the Metropolitan Anthony Bloom, who came to spend a day with us at All Nations Christian College, and many years later had led a Quiet Day for the Southwell Diocesan Evangelical Fellowship. Shortly after my discovery of the writings of the Archimandrite Sophrony, Bishop Kallistos Ware came to lead a Prayer Weekend at St. Peter's, Nottingham. I had known of him as Timothy Ware, whose book *The Orthodox Way* I had had on my shelves at home for some time. Later I came to understand and begin to appreciate ikons, especially Rublev's 'Old Testament Trinity', as it is sometimes called, a copy of which we had in St. Peter's.

In St. Peter's, Nottingham, with Canon Leslie Morley and Bishop Solomon Tilewa Johnson

In the meantime, my interest in overseas missions had not been forgotten. During my years at St. Peter's, I was much encouraged to join in their increasing involvement with the Church in Africa, first with a link in Mali, then with the Gambia through CMS Mission Partners, Malcolm and Gladys Millard whom I had known at St. Margaret's, Aspley. Bishop Solomon Tilewa Johnson, Bishop of the Gambia, came to visit us in Nottingham; the rector, Canon Leslie Morley, spent his sabbatical in Mali and the Gambia, and later a group from the parish went out on a visit to the Church in the Gambia. So mutual interest and prayer support increased. Later links with Uganda developed through a CMS doctor working there, and through Christian Aid with Sierra Leone - as there are several Sierra Leonians worshipping at St. Peter's. It was a great honour for me, when CMS held a commissioning service for new and returning Mission Partners at St. Peter's, to be asked to give the address.

My own contacts with Christians in Rwanda and Burundi continued, through correspondence and, increasingly, through visits which Rwandan Church leaders paid to this country for further study or conferences and consultations. Sometimes I was called in as interpreter, especially for wives of leaders whose English was not always good enough to follow what was being said. It was, however, a complete surprise in 1987 to receive a request from the bishops to write for them in the vernacular the history of how the Anglican Church began in Rwanda and Burundi. In Rwanda they had plans to hold a special Jubilee celebration in 1990 to mark the twenty-five years since they had their first Rwandan Bishop.

I realised this would necessitate a visit to East Africa, so, in consultation with the Ruanda Mission CMS, who generously agreed to cover the fare and expenses, I set off, in early 1988, for three months.

Chapter 11
Rwanda Revisited

The eighteen years that had elapsed since I last left Rwanda had inevitably brought about many changes; yet straightaway I felt 'at home'.

The Air France jet touched down on the runway of the new International Airport at Kigali, named 'Gregoire Kayibanda' after the first President of the Republique Rwandaise, in recognition of his contribution in the establishing of the Republic - and so named, significantly, by the then President, Major-General Juvénal Habyarimana, who had shared in the bloodless coup of 1973 that brought to power the MRND party (Mouvement Révolutionnaire National pour le Développement et la Démocratie) with Habyarimana himself as Rwanda's second President.

Walking down the gangway into the Customs Hall I wondered what my reception would be. I greeted the official who came along to examine my luggage in the vernacular. 'You know Kinyarwanda!' he exclaimed. 'Where did you learn?' As I recounted my various locations, he broke in, 'Shyira! That's my home!' And so we were well away with mutual memories - and he had even heard of me! 'Look,' he said, 'I'm supposed to tip all your luggage out,' (and I could see this happening to the other passengers), 'but just open your case so it looks as if I'm examining it.' Then he put his chalk sign on it and I was out into the reception area in no time. There I was hailed by a group of people led by Catherine, the Bishop's wife, and born off with much rejoicing to the waiting episcopal car!

As we drove along I was amazed at the transformation of Kigali, which as the capital of the country now had an impressive array of foreign embassies, a university and modern hotels for Rwanda had begun to build up a flourishing tourist trade. People came from many countries to visit the Game Parks, especially the now famous mountain gorilla of the Virunga Volcanic Range. Visitors also flew in from the Gulf States for the weekend to enjoy the cool refreshing climate. One day, Ted and Beryl Sisley, former colleagues who had made such a valuable contribution particularly to technical education in Rwanda, took me for lunch to a hotel in the Game Park near Gahini. We swam in the pool with elephants and giraffes browsing just outside the enclosure. Everywhere there seemed to

161

be an air of peace and stability and, indeed, throughout my journeyings I had no sense of the ethnic tensions of previous years. Though there had been outbreaks of violence against the Tutsis in the early '70s, it seemed mainly to be a reaction to Hutu being killed in Burundi, and this appeared to have died down as the MRND became established. Tutsis who had remained in the country had accepted the Republic and continued to work in education, hospitals, church or government offices, though they were a very small minority and not now in positions of authority. Those who had fled to Uganda and elsewhere appeared to have settled down and many found jobs, though most of them never lost the vision of returning 'home' one day, particularly those in Uganda who, during the years of civil disturbance under Amin and Obote, began to heed the cry, 'Rwandans go home!' Some Rwandans actively supported President Museveni, even fighting in his army, as he gradually subdued opposition forces and established a stable government. He in his turn was sympathetic to the cause of those seeking to return to Rwanda, and certainly did not discourage the formation of the RPF (Rwandan Patriotic Front) with its military force. But all this was embryonic when I was in these countries early in 1988, and in all my conversations with Rwandans I heard nothing indicative of the violence that was to erupt in the early '90s.

With Canon Eustace Kajuga, 1988

My brief was to write the history, in Kinyarwanda, of the Anglican Church in Rwanda, especially of the early years. Various books had been written for the English supporters of the Ruanda Mission, featuring the work of the missionary pioneers with brief mention of one or two of their more outstanding African colleagues, especially English-speaking ones. I was anxious, therefore, to talk with as many of the older Rwandan Christians as possible, particularly those who could remember the arrival of the first evangelists and missionaries.

With Marianne Kajuga, 1988

So, armed with my neat little tape-recorder, I set out for a most stimulating tour.

First I made myself known at the Kigali Diocesan Offices and was given assurance of enthusiastic support from the Diocesan Secretary (later Bishop) Onesephore Rwaje. Their records did not go back beyond the time of the independence of the EER (Église Épiscopale au Rwanda), but they directed me to the Literature Centre of the Protestant Alliance Churches just outside Kigali where I found one or two most interesting tape-recordings. One was a fairly recent interview with Bishop Kosiya Shalita (mentioned earlier), a Rwandan educated in Uganda who had accompanied the early missionaries into Rwanda and Burundi, and who later became Bishop of Mbarara in Uganda and the first Rwandan to be consecrated an Anglican Bishop.

For my travelling around the eastern part of Rwanda I was given the use of the diocesan car and a chauffeur, and found everywhere a great welcome and an eagerness to share memories of early days in the church, especially testimonies to the liberating power of the Gospel. Sometimes I talked with Bishops and Church leaders, but often with older retired church workers and members out on the hills. Sitting in the small front room of one quite humble dwelling with my little 'Sony' on the table between us, I recorded the story of the old man of the house, Simeon. He remembered the arrival of the two Ugandan evangelists in 1922, who started preaching the Gospel and teaching reading and writing. Simeon had been among the young men called by the local chief to go and 'learn' so that they would be able to read to him the communications that he received from time to time from the Belgian administrators and thus save him the embarrassment of it becoming known that he was illiterate! So, Simeon told me, he started with the reading, then as he listened to the teaching from the Word of God and later read it for himself, he came to a living faith in Christ, was baptised and eventually ordained. Several others with whom I talked mentioned other things that had first brought them into contact with the Gospel - some mentioned the 'tennisi' (tennis balls) which the white people gave to youngsters who attended classes regularly, and how as they listened the reality of what they heard about Jesus broke in on their hearts. Another, who later became a schoolmaster, had been herding his father's cattle in the bush country not far from Gahini when he heard a strange noise, 'piki-piki-piki-....' He hid behind a bush and saw a strange person with white skin riding on a sort of 'metal horse'. Captain Geoffrey Holmes, the rider of the motorbike, spotted the curious little head above the bush, stopped the bike and asked him if he'd like a ride. Boldly, he said he would! Geoff Holmes then told him about the school for boys he had started at Gahini, and suggested he ask his father if he could attend. He did, and was later baptised, taking the name 'Geoffrey' after Captain Holmes. He became a very committed Christian, a Canon and most able church worker until retirement in the late '80s when I was able to visit him and his wife Chloe in their nice brick house on the outskirts of Kigali.

Several of the people with whom I was anxious to speak were in Burundi, so I flew there and stayed in Bujumbura for a few days. My chief reason for going was to talk with Archbishop Sam Sindamuka, part of whose story I have already related. He had many memories of early contacts with the Church in Burundi, and also recollections of some of the missionary pioneers. I found it encouraging that he had begun to ordain women as deacons, and priests shortly after. He was ahead of the Rwandan bishops in this, believing that 'the church cannot go forward without their ministry.'

With Rev Erasto & Mrs Edreda Kinyogote at Gahini

Everywhere I went I met former pupils, men and women who had moved into positions of leadership. Others were Rwandans who had fled to Burundi during the expulsion of the Tutsis from Rwanda in the early '70s. Several of these were widows of former Church leaders, like Dorokasi, widow of Nikodemu Gatozi, one of the first ordained men in the Rwandan Church. He had been a clerk to the German officials in the Gahini area way back in the early years of the century, and then an official in the Belgian administration; when the Gospel had come to the area he had responded, and served tirelessly for many years. Then there was Hélène, one of the first of my pupils at the Shyira Teacher Training School, and one of the most able. Her husband, who worked at the hospital which served our large secondary school at Shyogwe, had been beheaded in front of her and her five-year-old daughter. Hélène herself had escaped with the smaller children, hiding in the millet field and eventually managing to get over the border into Burundi. Later she was able to rescue some of their cattle, and survived by selling milk and yoghurt and by cutting out and making garments for people around. From the first she had prayed for the conversion of those who had killed her husband, for they were pupils at our Shyogwe School and she knew them personally. One was soon apprehended and imprisoned, another was killed in a road accident, but the third she continued to remember in prayer. Eventually he came to repent of his crime, made a commitment to Christ and sought Hélène out in Bujumbura to ask her forgiveness. Her response to him was, 'I forgave you when you did it.'

Hélène and some of the others who had been in my Teacher Training School, and who had been particularly keen on the music and singing sessions, formed part of the 'Chorale' at the Anglican cathedral in Bujumbura, and on the Sunday I was there they sang some of the hymns and songs I had taught them years ago, the most memorable being a rendering in Kinyarwanda of Psalm 23 - *The Lord is my Shepherd* - set to 'Brother James's Air', which I found very moving.

Following the Burundi visit I flew back to Rwanda and then on by road into Uganda, stopping first for a few days at Kabale, where the Ruanda Mission had begun work in 1921, and met with an elderly lady who had been matron at the Girls' School run by Constance Hornby. It was Constance who had welcomed me to the school over forty years previously. Then I went in the hospital jeep to Kampala, stopping off at Mbarara, where I had a most moving talk with Bishop Erika Sabiti, who had been one of the early leaders in the East African Revival and who, from having suffered scorn and marginalisation from the clerical establishment of the time, eventually became the first African Archbishop of Uganda. When I met him he was very frail, but was delighted to see me and give a message on my tape-recorder for friends in England. His last words were, '...above all, remember this: keep your eyes on Jesus!' Three weeks later I heard that he had died.

In Kampala I enjoyed the hospitality of another of my former pupils, Esther Karimuzo. Her father, Erisa Rwabahungu, was one of the first three Rwandans to be ordained. He and his wife had left Rwanda during the '70s and settled on the Namutamba Tea Estate in Uganda, where he had later died. Namutamba, as already mentioned, had been a centre of the Revival and the base from which William Nagenda had worked. It had been established by the Lea-Wilson family who endeavoured to run the estate on Christian principles, with good conditions of service for the workers, many of whom were Rwandans. They had their own pastor, and services on Sundays were held in Kinyarwanda. From the beginning of racial tension in Rwanda in 1959 some leading members of the Anglican Church had settled there, and the reason for my visit was to talk with them. Several were close friends and former colleagues, including Mary Kanamuzeyi, widow of Pastor Yona who was murdered while ministering to refugees in the Bugesera. I found her still walking in quiet joyfulness with the Lord. Mostly I was anxious to talk to Canon John Bunyenyezi and his wife Marianne, a 'lay' Canon. We had worked together at Shyira and kept in close touch ever since. Originally from Bufumbira on the Uganda-Rwanda border, he had responded early to the Gospel and to the call to cross the border to share in the evangelisation of Rwanda. Selected for theological training at the Mukono Theological College in Uganda, he was one of the group (which included William Nagenda) of 'balokole' who were expelled from the college in 1941 for allegedly disobeying a request to stop holding excessive prayer meetings and early morning preaching at those whom they considered 'unsaved' among their fellow students. This had been a sad period in the history of the Ugandan Church, with misunderstandings and lack of communication on both sides, and I was so grateful to have been able to record John's first-hand account as he was, I believe, the only one of those involved who was still alive. Good too, to learn how later on much reconciliation had taken place between the 'balokole' students and the Church leaders.

Esther, with whom I was staying, had a spacious house, and during my stay with her drove me around in her car. Her husband had been a politician before joining the staff of Makerere University, but was murdered by Idi Amin leaving her also in danger, but she had been able to hide and eventually move back into her house. While she was a student (and one of the very brightest) at Shyogwe College, she had nothing to do with the Christian community, a situation which continued during later life; then following her husband's death she lapsed into alcoholism, suffering a terrible road accident through drunken driving, but while in hospital experienced a personal encounter with the Lord. Her life was transformed and she became quite a leader among the Christian women in Uganda. After her conversion she had written to me and her other tutors at college, to ask forgiveness for her bad behaviour there. An able business woman, she was running a boutique in Kampala, making regular trips to London for supplies. She was also a friend of Mrs. Museveni, the President's wife, helping her in her project for orphan children, of whom there were sadly thousands in Uganda after Amin's time, and also owing to Aids. It was a privilege to see first-hand how much the Christian people in Uganda were doing to help those in distress.

The remaining weeks of my research tour were spent mainly in the north and west of Rwanda, around the Shyira and Kigeme church centres. The Bishops in each place gave generously of their time, sharing their own memories of the earlier days and their vision for the future of the Church in their dioceses. Again I met former pupils, some now playing an important role in commerce, church or state. One, Isaac, who had helped me start the Girls' Training Class at Kigeme long ago, now offered me a car and chauffeur to travel wherever I liked; he also took me to the very interesting Museum in Butare, insisting on picking up the bill for the books I'd bought! Wherever I went the churches seemed to be growing fast, and there were plans, soon to be realised, of dividing each diocese into two or more, and forming a Province of Rwanda. I talked with people of both ethnic groups; they seemed to relate easily to each other and I had no indication of tensions there or in other spheres. Certainly, most of the leadership were of Hutu or mixed origin, which was not surprising considering the number of Tutsis who had fled in earlier years.

At Shyogwe it was a delight to enjoy renewed fellowship with Archdeacon Festo Gakware, another gracious man of God who had served the Church so faithfully for many years. He had been one of three Rwandan clergy who had come to England for a year's further training, with the idea that from among them would be chosen the first Bishop of Rwanda. In many ways Festo seemed the obvious choice, but the bench of Bishops in Uganda (in which Province we still were) had felt that his being a Tutsi might make it difficult for him in Republican Rwanda. Whether this would have been so can never be known, of course, but it has been wondered whether his appointment might not, in fact, have given the Church a more independent role in the country.

At Shyogwe also I was able to meet another long-term friend and colleague, Silas Kabirigi, a former schoolmaster still with the joyous Christian testimony with which I had first associated him. One of the first teachers to be trained by the Guillebauds in 1943, he had served at Shyogwe College and then been headmaster of the Primary School. In the 1959 outbreak of racial enmity he had been taken off to prison, beaten and left for dead under a pile of other bodies. Regaining consciousness, he crawled out in the night, and the guards had an awful fright in the morning to see him standing up reading from his New Testament. They thought he'd risen from the dead and let him go! However, back home again another group came along looking for cows to steal. 'You want my cows?' he said. 'Take them! When Jesus saved me I had no cows. He provided them for me, but they are not necessary for happiness, so you can take them.' 'Oh, let's go and get someone else's cows,' they said as they left!

Before returning to England, Bishop Adoniya of Kigali, the same who had encouraged me into Mothers' Union work years before, asked if I would consider taking over the directorship of the Church Secondary School at Gahini, as the Director then in post was leaving. To pray about this I went to a spot at the edge of the hill overlooking Lake Muhazi, drinking in the beauty of the country and realising how important this school would be to the Church. Yet was it the right move for me at this stage in life? I had realised as I'd talked with many people on my travels round the country how much things had changed from the land I knew. As I stood there I heard a voice deep in my heart, that I knew was the Lord's, saying, 'You don't belong here any more.' All my inner tension ceased, and I could say with conviction to the Bishop that this was no longer the Lord's place for me.

Back in England with all my cassettes, notes, photographs and memories, I set to work transcribing the tape-recordings, sorting material and planning the outline for the book. For some weeks I made regular visits to London to the Mission Headquarters to search through their archives. Reading through these and remembering the amazing testimonies I had heard, I was impressed yet again by the many answers to prayer experienced by so many down the years since the very clear guidance of God to those who began Anglican work in Rwanda and Burundi. Clearly, it seemed to me that the book should be called *The God Who Hears*; but during the course of a conversation with Peter Guillebaud, a brilliant Kinyarwanda linguist, he mentioned an old idiomatic phrase that might be used: 'Imana Igir'Amatwi', literally meaning 'God has ears.' However, in talking with some of the younger Rwandan leaders I found they were not familiar with the idiom, so eventually used the former title for the book.

I sent a transcript to Rwanda for their comments. Some of it was used in the 25 years' Jubilee Celebrations of the Église Épiscopale au Rwanda, and the whole book was in the process of being published when the political disturbances of the early '90s meant that nothing more was done and their copy seems to be lost. Recently I have been asked to revise it with a view to its being published, when it seems appropriate.

* * * * * * *

In 1991 the Bishop of Southwell, the Rt. Rev. Patrick Harris, himself a former missionary with the South American Missionary Society in Argentina, asked if I would take on the role of Diocesan Adviser in Overseas Relations from the Rev. Richard Kirton, who was moving to Sheffield to lecture at the Church Army Training College. I had for some time been a member of the Mission Group of the Diocesan Synod, and also of a group that Richard called together to increase awareness in the diocese of the World Church. The Group was made up of the Area Secretaries of the various Anglican Missionary Societies and other groups, such as Christian Aid, who worked overseas. We had already begun to plan a big event in Southwell Minster called 'A Celebration of World Mission' so the responsibility for implementing this now fell on me. Bishop Patrick had gladly agreed to lead the day, and he invited Bishop Michael Nazir-Ali, then General Secretary of CMS and later Bishop of Rochester, to give the 'keynote' and the final address. All the participating Societies ran workshops, there was a special programme for younger people, and we drew in overseas nationals studying or living here, to share in these events. Bishop Michael took the theme 'Jesus Christ, the Light of the World', and the whole event was most encouraging, with many parishes represented and the involvement of people from other countries helping everyone to realise the vibrance of other churches around the world.

The Southwell Partnership for World Mission (as we now called our group of Mission Representatives) continued to meet at my home, and we grew in fellowship and understanding of one another's ministry and areas of interest. Rather than hold another big central World Mission event, I began to work on the idea of more local World Mission weekends, discussing this with the Rural Deans. Beginning with the Mansfield Deanery we circulated all the parishes with information. A general meeting was held on the Saturday afternoon in one of the parish halls, with worship, workshops for adults and children, and talks. A shared meal divided the two main sessions, so people from different parishes could meet each other and the visitors from overseas - mostly students in theological colleges in Nottingham or Birmingham. On the Sunday morning the team of speakers, which included the overseas students, divided up to preach in several different parishes in the Deanery. This pattern of sharing World Mission interest proved so popular that we repeated it in other deaneries, and it has continued under my successor, Bishop Bill Flagg, who moved to Southwell Deanery on retiring as General Secretary of SAMS.

At a Thanksgiving Celebration, Southwell Minster, 1990 – 50 years after signing the 'pledge'; with [left to right] Josephine Stancliffe, Jean & David Ward (Vicar of St. Margaret's, Aspley) and Elizabeth Waters, a missionary friend.

During the three and a half years as Overseas Adviser, I was Bishop's Nominee on the Council of USPG, attending their residential conferences at High Leigh near All Nations Christian College, which gave me opportunities of keeping in touch with the staff there. Again, sharing in the mission of USPG and getting to know other Council members further enriched my experience of the faith, ministry and spirituality of those with a different theological background. I also soon discovered that some of their leaders and members were much nearer my own tradition than I had imagined! I became, and still am, an 'incorporated member' of USPG as well as being a member and Vice-President of CMS.

At the end of 1992 I moved house again (the twentieth move of my adult life!) and settled just outside Southwell. I had had no thoughts of moving from my little OAP-type bungalow, but one day Bishop Patrick had called in to discuss final details and pray about the Celebration of World Mission day we were planning. So much was packed into what was virtually a bed-sit, and I remarked in passing that I could do with an extra room. But I thought no more about this until one evening a month or so later when I had a phone call from him. 'Doreen, you know when I came to your little home you said how you would like something bigger? Well, there's a flat going just outside Southwell. Why not come and see it?' I accordingly fixed a date, and his wife Valerie, who was a Trustee of the small Trust that administered the block of four flats, took me to see it. The setting was delightful, with farmland around and about a mile from the Minster. The flats had been left to the Diocese for 'retired clergy and church workers who had been in this or Derby Diocese for ten years or more' - and it was rent-free! Not wishing to let this latter point sway me, I considered the pros and cons, and consulted various friends. Everyone seemed to feel it would be a good move, but I hesitated because I was daunted by the thought of yet another move. I prayed for clear guidance, especially that someone else would take the flat, but there seemed to be no-one else eligible who wanted it. Then I prayed about my future ministry. Would there be opportunities in Southwell for this? Quite 'by chance' I met the Provost, the Very Rev. David Leaning, as I was walking by the Minster Office, and told him about the situation. We arranged a time to talk and pray, and he said how welcome I would be to share in ministry in the Minster, and have my Reader's Licence transferred there. I discovered there was a bus running through Southwell from Nottingham to Newark, so I went on it to explore the market town of Newark, finding it a most interesting historic place with pleasant river front by the Castle ruins. The next Sunday I drove over to the Minster for the morning service - it was an official service for the Queen's birthday - and as I sat in the side aisle, the main nave being so crowded, I felt the Lord was saying, 'How much louder do I have to speak? The Bishop rings you up, those you trust feel it's the right move, there's a welcome to ministry here in the Minster, and it's rent-free!' Outside after the service I was given an encouraging welcome by the Bishop, so, with a sense of peace, I notified the Treasurer that I would like to accept the tenancy. Renovations took some months, but just before Christmas 1992 I moved into Upton Fields Flats - beginning a new sphere of ministry at Southwell. In the years that followed – particularly as there have been some difficult times - I have been so thankful for the very clear guidance I received on making the move from Nottingham.

* * * * * * *

During my fourth year as Overseas Mission Adviser to Southwell Diocese, I felt that the time had come to hand over to someone who could give a higher profile to Overseas Mission than could an elderly spinster! So eventually Bishop Bill Flagg took on the role, and I realised the importance of seeking the Lord's pattern for another new stage in life.

Living alone with few outside commitments could, I thought, provide special opportunity for prayer, meditation and intercession - to which I had felt a specific call on several occasions in the past. I had felt a yearning to follow the Psalmist who says (in Psalm 119:164), *'Seven times a day do I praise thee.'* And I'd made attempts to do this as far as my hitherto busy programme allowed. Now I hoped that I might make this a Rule, as it were, for the next stage of the journey - not to be straitjacketed by it, but using it as a Spirit-directed framework. It was about this time that I heard of the Fellowship of Solitaries, a prayer fellowship of those seeking to follow a calling to inner solitude and prayer. I joined this Fellowship, and receive their helpful newsletter and updated membership list three times a year. The daily pattern that I seek to follow (with adaptations from time to time) is:

1. On waking - a brief meditation on a Bible verse, or Radio 4's Thought for the Day.

2. Around 9 am - Morning Prayer using ASB (or other) Lectionary readings, with prayer focus on those in ministry in the UK with whom I have special links. When possible, on Mondays and Saturdays, Holy Communion at 9 am in the Minster.

3. Mid-morning - Praise for 5-10 minutes, or Radio 4 Daily Service.

4. Lunch-time - Intercessions. A longer time with focus on the World Church, praying for those individuals and concerns known to me, as well as other general prayer cycles.

5. Mid-afternoon - 5-10 minutes Quiet, or using the 'Jesus Prayer'.

6. Evening - Evening Prayer, using the Lectionary readings, with prayer focus on family, friends and special requests.

7. Bedtime - prayers, with focus on members of the Fellowship of Solitaries.

The times in between form 'units' for gardening, writing and other activities.

I shared my hopes to follow this 'Rule' with several friends and with Bishop Patrick. He was most encouraging and agreed to 'commission' me to this pattern of prayer, and to the Fellowship of Solitaries at a service in his private chapel. He celebrated Holy Communion, laid hands on me and prayed for this new ministry. Some friends who were able to join me also prayed. Afterwards we all shared a meal together at the invitation of John Watson, a fellow Reader at the Minster, and his wife Gwyneth, in their flat at Bishop's Manor. It was a very special time.

Chapter 12
Hope for the future

'But - it's so beautiful!' commented my companions with amazement, as we journeyed from the Uganda border westward across Rwanda. It was early July 1996, and for two years the horrors of the 1994 genocide and consequent disruption of daily life had rarely been absent from the world's media. It was hard to reconcile the beauty and seeming peacefulness of those spectacular hills and valleys with the horrific pictures we had all absorbed from our TV screens. As was also the sight of people busy cultivating in the valleys and picking tea on the hillsides, carrying their produce to the crowded markets, and rebuilding ruined buildings. This called forth another comment, 'But they're so energetic!' Indeed, the first impression was one of hope and planning for a peaceful future - though we were to find, on closer contact with people, hidden pain and underlying apprehension. There were road checks along the way, with soldiers in evidence near the larger centres and crossroads, but we were treated with the utmost courtesy and hardly stopped once our jeep was recognised as that of the Bishop of Kigeme, Norman Kayumba, in whose Diocese we were to stay for two weeks.

On the steps of Kigali Cathedral, 1996

'We' were a team of four: a South African Archdeacon, a lady from Scotland who was a member of the General Synod of the Scottish Episcopal Church, a chaplain for the Inter-continental Church Society living in Monaco, and myself. We were part of a larger international team from fourteen countries (from New Zealand to Newfoundland!), under the auspices of SOMA (Sharing of Ministries Abroad), an international Christian fellowship with a special ministry of encouraging understanding of the work of the Holy Spirit in healing and reconciliation. The Anglican Church leaders in Rwanda had invited SOMA to send a team to help them seek the Lord's pattern for their ministry to Rwanda in the time ahead. Team members were those who had experience of situations of racial or political tension, or who had teaching, pastoral and linguistic gifts. My own inclusion was very much a last-minute decision, though surely a God-directed one when I consider all the answers to prayer which dispersed the obstacles to my taking part in such a project at short notice.

I had flown out to Africa with other members of the UK team, including Beryl Sisley, who had also joined the party at the last minute. Team members from other countries joined us in Nairobi, where we spent an interesting Sunday joining in the very lively Cathedral service there and meeting some Bishops from the Sudan. The next lap of the journey was by bus to Kampala, passing the spectacular scenery over the escarpment and Rift Valley and bringing back memories of holiday visits to Kenya in earlier years.

Don Brewin, the Director of SOMA (UK), joined us in Kampala as he had been on a mission to Zaire (now the Democratic Republic of Congo). We spent some days meeting and getting to know the other team members, and in prayer, worship and orientation at Makerere University, hosted by the University chaplain, Canon Benoni Mugarura-Mutana, who with his wife Joyce accompanied us to Rwanda. We were very well looked after at the Lion Hotel in Kampala, where I, being the oldest member of the group, was given one of the few single rooms! In Kampala I noticed how much restoration had gone on since my visit in 1988 when there were still signs of the devastation caused by the civil war. Buildings had been repaired and roads mended. Unfortunately I did not manage to get up to Namirembe Hill, where I had so often stayed in the past, but I was able to talk with Archbishop Livingstone Nkoyoyo, who had stayed with me in Nottingham when I was CMS Area Secretary and he a CMS 'Exchange Visitor'.

At last the day came for the journey into Rwanda. We made an early start from the hotel to catch a bus for the long journey to Kigali. Stopping for breakfast at Masaka, the news leaked out that it was my birthday, so 'Happy Birthday' was sung as we stood sipping our coffee in the bus station! Lunch at Mbarara was much more sumptuous and fortified us well for the dust and bumps of the last part of the route to the frontier. Here we had a lengthy wait, as dealing with over thirty people of so many nationalities, most of whom needed interpreters, could not be hurried! Meanwhile, feeling as though I was home again, I had several interesting chats with local bystanders, some of whom turned out to be Christians from a nearby village. They told me of the blessings which were spreading around and of increasing congregations. One young man, hearing I was a teacher, said, 'Won't you stay, please, we need teachers so badly.'

A wonderful welcome awaited us at Kigali, with speeches and substantial refreshments. Bishop Onesephore Rwaje, then the acting Dean of the Province, told us of the programme we were to follow, and introduced the hosts of the various places where we were going for our first week in groups of four or five. I received warm hugs from several of the welcome party with whom I had worked years ago. I was surprised when Bishop Norman also hugged and hugged me, as I did not think I had known him. 'Oh, it's so good to see you again!' he said, then turning to those around us, he announced, 'She was the Directrice of our school when I was in Year Two, and she started our Mothers' Union!' Then he ushered Mary, Chris, Peter and me (the Kigeme team) into his car and we set off across country. After supper in his house we were escorted to our sleeping places. Mary and I were housed in what had once been my guest house, which we had called 'Inzu y'amahoro' ('the House of Peace'). How welcome it was to see a log fire burning (Kigeme is 7,000 ft up on the edge of the high rainforest) and drop into bed. 'Tomorrow we make an early start,' Bishop Norman had said, 'as we are going to a church centre two hours journey away.'

The visit was to Nkomero, in the high hills near the forest, one of the districts where I had founded Primary Schools some forty years before. Memories of those 'safaris' when I had tramped the hillsides, camped out in my little tent, measured out the sites for schools, and gathered possible teachers together, all flooded back! I remembered the progress we made, from the children learning first in the mud-and-wattle church building with no doors or windows, and then as the need for more classrooms grew, simple thatched roof structures were put up, sun-dried brick walls being built later. I could picture the children sitting on logs or benches made of bricks, and learning to write first of all in the dust until I could manage to provide slates then exercise books out of our limited resources. How long ago that all was - yet how close it seemed to me!

Several of the buildings at Nkomoro had been vandalised in the war, but the roofs were still intact on most of them and the bare walls were still standing. I was surprised at the number of local people who recognised me and were so warm in their greetings. People from all over the country were so grateful that we should have bothered to come from our own homes especially to visit them. Sometimes they felt the outside world had forgotten them. I heard stories of violent deaths, of relatives imprisoned though seemingly innocent, and was amazed at the acceptance of tragedy and the spirit of hope shown by those of a committed Christian faith. Likewise we were all amazed at the big open-air Sunday meetings the Bishop had organised, at the sense of praise and joy of the worshippers, many having walked miles or even stayed somewhere overnight on the way there. Many were young people under sixteen (and we found them in all the churches we visited) who had formed themselves into 'Chorales' with a repertoire of hymns, often composed by themselves and using actions, based on Bible verses and set to tunes of their own composition. Apparently they met during the week to pray and choose the theme for their contribution on the Sunday. It was difficult to realise, as one looked round on their smiling faces, that many if not all of them had witnessed the most terrible atrocities and lost several relatives and friends.

We held a teaching session after the main meetings, for pastors and other leaders, but many other people crowded in as well, not wishing to miss anything! We heard that soldiers had been called to patrol and guard the area of our meeting, as disturbances had been reported further up towards the forest where some of the former militia responsible for the genocide had infiltrated from the Congo. All was peaceful, however, while we were there. More disturbing was the manifestation of demonic activity among some of those attending the meetings. Mary and I took some of these outside as they were causing a disturbance, and prayed with them. Two women in particular showed signs of demonic possession, and we prayed in the Name of Jesus, commanding the spirit to leave. One woman did seem to be really set free, but I felt uneasy about the other, and indeed she returned the next day and was finally set free also. Several others asked for help as they said they felt an 'oppression', and after questioning admitted they had resorted to native healers and worn charms to protect from witchcraft even though as Christians they had known this was not right. It seemed that across the country, especially in the remoter areas, there had been a turning back to pre-Christian practices, and church leaders have not always known how to deal with this. Part of our ministry was to help these leaders to see the biblical way of bringing help and deliverance to such people.

Back at Kigeme itself we held morning and afternoon sessions for clergy and evangelists - some of whom were very able women - teaching them the biblical exercise of the 'gifts of the Spirit' as some of them were experiencing pressure from extreme pentecostalist pastors who sometimes accused them of not being true Christians because they did not exercise the gifts of prophecy or healing or other gifts in the same way. We had helpful Bible studies and listened to their questions; in one of the sessions the Spirit led us into a time of ministry to one another for healing and release in different ways.

I was encouraged to see all the building that had gone on since my visit in 1988: a fine Diocesan Centre with up-to-date office equipment, and a large Evangelists' Training School - which was used in our second week to house representatives of all the Dioceses for the large conference we held when the rest of our international team joined us. For that occasion the Bishop had built special kitchen facilities in which the Mothers' Union members provided excellent meals for us all. As I had started the Mothers' Union work at Kigeme, it was a particular joy to see their quiet efficiency and the constructive role they were playing in the church and country generally. The Girls' Secondary School I had established so long ago had developed beyond recognition. It was hard to recognise our original classrooms as so many other buildings had been packed on to the fairly restricted hilltop site. It was also encouraging to hear that there was a very lively Christian Union (the school was now under government control, and co-educational) with pupils meeting regularly for prayer and Bible study. I was able to meet a group of these on the Sunday afternoon and hear their testimonies and gather something of the influence they had on the general atmosphere of the school. Many of them had suffered bereavements, and some students had been killed at home or on their way to school though none in the actual school buildings.

On our first day there I had several visitors who remembered me and came to greet me and tell me their stories. One was an elderly lady who brought me a gift of passion fruit, which she could have sold for much needed cash in the market. It was hard to recognise her as the young housegirl who used to help us with chores. She wanted to thank me for what the experience of our training and care had meant, and how it had helped her in later life. Her recent story was typical of so many that I was to hear. 'They came,' she said, speaking of the killers, 'took our family and destroyed everything. My husband fled and I waited for them to come back and kill me, putting myself in God's hands - but they went by! My husband also returned safely. Now we just manage to scratch a living from a small patch of ground, and the Lord is with us.' Later she told me, 'We have learned that we must love those who did these things, and, as God does with us, hate the sin but love the sinner.' I marvelled at the confident faith of this simple, barely literate women, in such circumstances.

One afternoon, when the rest of our team had joined us, we went to the place the Rwandan authorities have set aside as a memorial to those slaughtered in the surrounding area. A former large training centre

At a SOMA pre-Lambeth Conference, 1998

(nearby which I had once established a primary school) had been turned into a mortuary, made up of former classroom after classroom full of skeletons, of children as well as adults, exhumed from the pits into which they had been thrown and laid out for the world to see the visual evidence of the horrors of the genocide. We walked round in silence from room to room, gathering afterwards for a time of prayer at the special 'memorial grave'. Many of our group were deeply moved to tears, and indeed it was a fearsome sight. For myself, knowing that several of my friends' and fellow-workers' skeletons lay there, I remembered their radiant faith and testimonies, and seemed to 'see' them now, rejoicing before the Lamb with that great 'cloud of witnesses' from throughout the ages. It was an unforgettable and most solemn time.

During the week, as we met with Diocesan representatives, we heard more and more stories of the Lord's upholding in horrific happenings - sometimes miraculous escapes, or examples of outstanding courage as people protected those of the other ethnic group at great risk of personal harm or even death. Realising that many of these leaders and certainly many in their congregations would still be suffering from the trauma and repressed grief of all they had been through, we gave teaching and personal counselling about this. I remembered especially the family of a former colleague of mine, a much respected headmaster and leader of the Boys' Brigade. He, a Hutu, was married to a Tutsi lady; his first wife, also a Tutsi, had died long before, and he had grown-up children, some of them living in Europe, as well as young children from his second marriage. As a Christian he had refused to take part in the killings, then the militia had come to him saying, 'If you don't come and join with us in getting rid of the Tutsis, we will kill your wife.'

'I'm sorry,' he had replied, 'but I cannot join in with or condone what is wrong before God.' So they killed his wife and younger children, and finally killed him. I could not help but wonder what would be the reaction of many of us in England if faced with such a situation. This kind of threat had been made to many with mixed marriages, including some senior Church leaders.

Our last few days in Rwanda were spent back in Kigali, meeting with other leaders and ending with a moving service in the Cathedral. There I remembered my friend and former student at All Nations College, Alphonse Karuhije, Dean of Kigali Cathedral, who was murdered there after courageously refusing to flee the country, and prayed again for his wife Thaciènne and family living in exile but maintaining a strong testimony to God's enabling grace.

Staying in the Diocesan Guest House meant that I received many visitors from the city and surrounding area. Some were former refugees of the 1960s who had now returned from years in Uganda, but others came who had stayed on and borne witness to the oneness we have in Christ across all divisions. Teams of both ethnic groups were going out at weekends to different areas around sharing the message of reconciliation in Christ. 'We have asked each other's forgiveness,' they would say, 'for the evils our ethnic group has done to the other, and meet in forgiveness at the Cross. We beseech you, in Christ's Name, to do the same.'

Near Kigali there is a church building kept as a memorial to the unity of Christians in Christ. One Sunday during the genocide of 1994, a band of militia approached the church while the service was in progress, and called on the Hutu present to come out as all the Tutsi were going to be killed. The Hutu refused, saying, 'We no longer recognise those distinctions. We aren't Hutu, or Tutsi, we're Christians - and Rwandans.' The militia wiped out the whole congregation.

In a small rather dark house on the Diocesan compound, I had lunch with two of my oldest friends and colleagues, Geoffrey and Chloe Kinyanza. (He is the Geoffrey mentioned earlier who began his journey to faith with a ride on pioneer missionary Geoffrey Holmes' motor-bike.) In 1988 I had visited them in their nice brick house just outside Kigali, and it was here in 1994 that the perpetrators of genocide found them, hacked Geoffrey down, beating him cruelly and slashing him with knives. They locked the door, took the key, and dragged Chloe off towards the main place of execution in the city. However, at a junction of the paths, the soldier holding her whispered, 'Slip back down that path home,' and let her go! Arriving back at the house she found the neighbours gathered, saying, 'We can't leave the Canon unburied in there.' They managed to batter down the door, and found Geoffrey wasn't dead! Careful nursing restored him to life, though he remained weak and fairly immobile. They were both so peaceful in spite of what had happened to them and the fact that their son and other relatives had been killed, and reiterated what they had already written to me after their tragedy, 'We have no bitterness, we only pray that those who did these things may come to know the joy of Jesus.'

I also met up again with Hélène and some of her family. She had returned from Burundi and was settled in Kigali where her small house was refuge to many widows and orphans. 'How do you manage to feed them all?' I asked. 'It is the Lord's doing,' she replied. 'We never know where the next supplies will come from, but we trust our loving Lord.'

Several people said such things as the following: 'When the worst you can possibly imagine has happened and God has been there, you are then not afraid of anything else that may happen. We look with hope to the future with Him.' Another young woman whose husband and children were killed and all her possessions taken, said, 'When you have lost everything and have nothing left but Jesus, you discover that all you need is Jesus.' Such testimonies humbled and challenged me deeply.

Another visitor was Modeste Mudaheranwa, my secretary when I was Schools Inspector and to whom I handed on that role when I became the Mothers' Union worker. He had steadily refused to have anything to do with the 'ethnic cleansing' though he knew his life was often in danger. He told moving stories of how the Lord had over-ruled in several instances, and added, 'All this trauma brought me to a living faith that I did not really have before. In fact, I can say that I have been born again through these terrible happenings.'

Several children of former colleagues came to greet me and introduce their own families. Many had testimonies to the Lord's upholding. Josephine, a nurse at Kigali hospital and daughter of one of my school managers, came to share her story. Racially, she was half-Hutu, half-Tutsi, as were so many, but looked rather more Tutsi. She had been seized in the street by three men who put a machete to her throat. 'I felt the power of God come upon me,' she told me, 'and I grabbed the handle of the machete and said, "By the authority of the Name of Jesus, do not do this wicked thing!"' The men looked startled, dropped the machete and slunk away, letting her go free! Weeks later, when the Rwanda Patriotic Front had gained control, she met one of the men in the street. On recognising her, he started to cower away. But, 'I put my hand on his arm,' she said, 'and told him, "Don't be afraid, I'm not going to turn you in to the authorities. You didn't hurt me."' Then, noticing how ill he was looking, she said, 'Oh, you don't look well.' 'No,' he replied, 'I've been feeling ill for some time.' 'Well,' she told him, 'I'm a nurse - come over to the hospital and I'll help you.'

Again, at Kigeme, one of our former gardener/woodcutters had run after me to greet me on the road to the church. He recounted something of the horror of those days in 1994, of the raiding and the looting. Himself a Hutu he had refused to join in, as indeed was the case with many, many of them. 'They came up to the edge of the compound, intent on sacking the hospital,' he told me, 'but *we* weren't having any of it and wouldn't let them come!' Indeed, I saw that the hospital doors and windows were still in place, though very sadly some workers had been killed and so standards had fallen badly, though the young Rwandan doctor in charge was doing his best to build things up again.

After our week of prayer, study and sharing, as well as most inspiring times of worship, the Church leaders drew up a statement of what they all thought God was saying to them, a summary of which was that:

- the Church must not take sides, but condemn evil from whatever quarter it comes;
- the Church must enable Christians to be channels of the redeeming love of Christ, loving the sinner while condemning the sin;
- the Church must move out in compassion to all those who suffer, of whatever ethnic group, and minister in the power of the Spirit in healing and reconciliation.

They requested that we encourage the Church around the world to pray for them as they prepared for the way ahead.

From the days of the East African Revival the watchword of the Church in Rwanda had been 'one in Christ.' This was its strong point, and is the foundation of the Church's ongoing work of reconciliation in a country which was torn apart by ethnic conflict. Theirs is the living reality that in Christ Jesus there is neither Jew nor Gentile, Catholic or Protestant, male or female, Hutu or Tutsi; but that they are all one in the Spirit of Christ.

We left Kigali by bus for Kampala and the plane home - again a difficult and dusty journey with long tedious delays, especially at the Rwanda frontier post owing to our numbers and different nationalities. When it came to my turn to go into the passport office, I greeted the officials in Kinyarwanda. 'What have you all been doing during this visit?' they asked. 'We've been sharing the Good News of the love of God shown to us through Jesus Christ,' I replied. 'Then, why aren't you sharing it with us?' they questioned. 'All right,' I said, and was just starting to do so when the senior official suggested we go outside to talk. One or two others joined us in the compound outside, where a crowd of other people and some soldiers were gathered. So I talked to them in more detail about what Jesus had done for us on the Cross to reconcile us to God and to each other. After talking for a while, the passport official finally said, 'Yes, you are right - there is no hope for our land except in that way.'

Others in the crowd murmured agreement. 'Please ask people to pray for us,' were the last words I heard as I walked on across the border to Uganda.

Epilogue

'And I shall dwell in the house of the Lord for ever.'

As I have looked back over these pages, I've realised that a considerable number of those whose stories I have told have already passed into the Lord's unclouded Presence, some indeed, especially in Rwanda, since we began editing the book for publication. I was reminded of a comment made by a former missionary colleague at a Thanksgiving Service for another fellow missionary: 'The reception party is growing larger and larger up there!' - and indeed it is. But I have also noticed that towards the end of their lives, when people may be less able to cope with adversity, there have often been bewildering trials and other circumstances, pain, sorrow and suffering, especially for those who appear to have experienced great triumphs and accomplished much for God's Kingdom and seen wonderful answers to prayer - and this can be hard to understand. Corrie ten Boom, who for the last five years of her life could neither move nor speak, used to say that through these things God is training us for our unknown ministry, here on earth or beyond.

The completion of this book has been delayed by unexpected happenings. One joyous one for me was my sudden and unexpected visit to Rwanda in 1996, which occupied not only the weeks of the actual voyage but several weeks afterwards as I was asked to speak in various places and write about it. A different interruption occurred when I slipped on an icy path at the very end of the year, sustaining a complicated fracture of my femur and necessitating several weeks in hospital and months of limited activity. Contrary to what I would have expected, I didn't find it easy to read or pray in these circumstances, or to attend to the serious completion of this book. The year 1998 seemed to offer hope for real progress, then in the spring I discovered a lump beneath my right breast. Hospital visits, tests, and biopsy confirmed that it was cancer. Again, the emotional reaction to this seemed, to my shame, to paralyse my thinking for a while. But I know that around the world prayer has been made for me in many churches and groups, and the treatment I have been receiving (as part of a clinical research programme to test the efficacy and long-term effects of two different hormone tablets) has so far been successful, with no ill effects so far though I shall continue to be monitored for another year or so. Up to now it has been a positive outcome to a negative situation. But during this time Corrie ten Boom's words have reassured me again that nothing should be wasted, but received as God's pruning, shaping and training for future ministry, whether in this life or the next. So I have again committed myself to my pattern of prayer and intercession, including time to listen to God, that I may be open to His preparation 'to dwell in the House of the Lord for ever.'

D. J. Peck
15 Kings Court,
Southwell,
NG25 0EL
August 1999

At All Nations Christian College Silver Jubilee Celebrations, April 1997

Chronology

1919	- Doreen Peck born
	- Ruanda-Urundi mandated to Belgium under the League of Nations
1922	- Anglican evangelists and schoolmasters from Uganda entered Eastern Ruanda (temporarily under British administration)
1925	- First CMS Ruanda Mission centre established at Gahini, Ruanda
1926	- First Anglican baptisms in Ruanda, at Gahini
1930	- CMS Ruanda Mission granted 'Personnalité Civile' by the Belgians
1933	- First Revival Convention, at Kabale, Uganda
1935	- Alliance of Protestant Missions formed for Ruanda-Urundi
1940	- First Diocesan Council formed for the Anglican Church of Ruanda-Urundi and Kigezi, Uganda
1941	- First ordinations of African clergy in Ruanda
1946	- Silver Jubilee of Ruanda Mission CMS
	- Ruanda Mission signs Education Agreement with the Government
1947	- DP arrives in Ruanda
1951	- Consecration in Westminster Abbey of first Assistant Bishop (Bishop Jim Brazier) of Uganda, to have sole responsibility for Archdeaconry of Kigezi and Ruanda-Urundi
1959	- Death of King Mutara Rudahigwa of Ruanda
	- First outbreak of politico-ethnic violence (Parmehutu party)
1961	- Ruanda declared a Republic, with largely Hutu Government
1962	- Independence granted to Rwanda and Burundi
1965/6	- Formation of separate independent Diocese of Rwanda and Burundi, having their own African Bishops (Bishop Adoniya Sebununguri and Bishop Yohana Nkunzumwami)
1966	- Beginning of 'partnership' years between Ruanda Mission CMS and the African Church in Rwanda
1967	- DP inaugurates Mothers' Union officially in Rwanda
1970	- DP's return to England, to lecture at All Nations Christian College
1971	- Ruanda Mission's 50-year Jubilee
1973	- Fulfilment of Ruanda Mission: full autonomy of African Church in Rwanda and Burundi
	- After more than 10 years of sporadic outbreaks of ethnic violence, Rwandan Army Chief of Staff, Major General Juvénal Habyarimana, seizes power (MRND Party - Mouvement Révolutionnaire National pour le Développement et la Démocratie)
1978	- DP appointed CMS Area Secretary for the Dioceses of Sheffield and Southwell
1980	- Formation of Francophone Anglican Province of Rwanda, Burundi and Zaire, under Archbishop Bezalel Ndahura of Zaire

1982	- DP 'retirement' in Nottingham: Administrator at St. Margaret's, Aspley, then Pastoral Assistant at St. Peter's, Nottingham
1988	- DP visits Rwanda, Burundi and Uganda to carry out research for a book, in the vernacular, on the growth of the Anglican Church in Rwanda
1991	- DP appointed Adviser in Overseas Relations for Southwell Diocese
	- From early '90s, Tutsi exiles in Uganda form RPF (Rwanda Patriotic Front) and re-enter Rwanda. Training of Hutu militia (Interahamwe) in Rwanda to resist them.
1992	- Anglican Province of Rwanda inaugurated, on 7th June, under Archbishop Augustin Nshamihigo (Bishop of Shyira)
1993	- Peace Accord signed in Arusha, Tanzania, after months of negotiations
1994	- President Habyarimana killed in plane crash; murder suspected. Genocide sweeps the country, instigated by the Interahamwe
	- RPF eventually gain control; ethnically 'mixed' Government established, under President Pasteur Bizimungu
1996	- DP revisits Rwanda with SOMA team, at invitation of Rwandan Bishops

Bibliography

Harold Adeney, *Light is Come*, Ruanda Mission CMS, (undated)
Harold Adeney, *Only One Weapon*, Ruanda Mission CMS, 1963
Amy Carmichael, *Gold by Moonlight*, SPCK, 1935
Amy Carmichael, *Toward Jerusalem*, SPCK, 1936
J. E. Church and Colleagues of the Ruanda Mission CMS,
    Forgive Them: The Story of an African Martyr
    (Yona Kanamuzeyi), Hodder & Stoughton, 1966
J. E. Church, *Quest for the Highest*, Paternoster Press, 1981
Lindesay Guillebaud, *A Grain of Mustard Seed: The Growth of the Ruanda
    Mission of CMS*,   Ruanda Mission CMS, 1959
Catherine James, *Africa Road*, Ruanda Mission CMS, (undated)
Fergal Keane, *Season of Blood - A Rwandan Journey*, Viking, 1995
Ian Linden, *Church and Revolution in Rwanda*, Manchester UP, 1977
Hugh McCullum, *The Angels Have Left Us*, WCC Publications, 1994
Jocelyn Murray, *Proclaim the Good News - A Short History of the Church
    Missionary Society*, Hodder & Stoughton, 1985
H. H. Osborn, *Fire in the Hills*, Highland Books, 1991
H. H. Osborn, *Revival, A Precious Heritage*, Apologia Publications, 1995
Patricia St. John, *Breath of Life*, The Norfolk Press, 1971
M. Basilea Schlink, *God is Always Greater*, The Faith Press, 1963
A. C. Stanley Smith, *Road to Revival - The Story of the Ruanda Mission*,
    CMS, 1946 (Supplement, 1951)
A.C. Stanley Smith, *An African Nebuchadnezzar - The Story of a Ruanda
    Chief*, Ruanda Mission CMS, (undated)
Corrie ten Boom, *Tramp for the Lord*, Hodder & Stoughton, 1974
John Tyndale-Biscoe, *Behind the Rectory Door - Come On In*, Avon Books, 1995
G. Jan van Butselaar, *'Christian Conversion in Rwanda: The Motivations'*,
    International Bulletin of Missionary Research, Vol 5, No 3,
    July 1981